Seasons Celebrate

August to December

Written by Ann Richmond Fisher

Illustrated by Becky J. Radtke

Teaching & Learning Company

1204 Buchanan St., P.O. Box 10
Carthage, IL 62321-0010

This book belongs to

_____

Cover art by Becky J. Radtke

Cover design by Jennifer Morgan

Copyright © 2003, Teaching & Learning Company

ISBN No. 1-57310-383-7

Printing No. 987654321

Teaching & Learning Company
1204 Buchanan St., P.O. Box 10
Carthage, IL 62321-0010

Before offering any food to your students, make sure you are aware of any allergies or dietary restrictions your students may have.

At the time of publication every effort was made to insure the accuracy of the information included in this book. However, we cannot guarantee that agencies and organizations mentioned will continue to operate or to maintain these current locations.

Table of Contents

August

September

October

November

December

Dear Teacher or Parent,

Congratulations on choosing the best one-stop seasonal resource ever! Packed inside this volume is a huge assortment of learning activities, bulletin board ideas, recipes and everything you need to celebrate lots of special days from August to December.
This book will supply you with material for many, many special days from back-to-school to Christmas. In addition to all the major holidays such as Halloween and Thanksgiving, we've also included helps for other special occasions that are just as fun but not as celebrated. For instance, wouldn't your students just love to observe Elephant Appreciation Day, watermelon festivals and the discovery of the South Pole?

While your primary students are enjoying holidays and special observances, they will also be practicing important skills in language, math and other subjects. You'll find many skill-based reproducibles inside that are ready to use. The wide variety of formats used includes puzzles, matching, creative writing, word searches and more. Most require no special supplies or equipment. Additionally, you'll find bulletin board ideas, shape book patterns, party suggestions, parent letters, recipes, songs, poems and much, much more.

An extra-unique feature of this book is the CD-Rom. This helpful aid is packed with lots of whimsical clip art to complement the material inside the book. The clip art is made available in both black-and-white and color and can easily be sized to fit your needs—from name tags, to book covers to special projects. You will also find patterns for bulletin boards, theme-decorated stationery and much, much more! And everything is numbered for easy-use and reference.

This large volume is divided into five monthly sections. Most months feature six special occasions. There are language and math pages for each occasion as well as other skill-based materials. Each month includes two or three bulletin board ideas that are complete with patterns and display ideas. Near the end of each monthly section, you'll find award certificates and bookmarks for the units in that month. At the back of the book, you'll also find a handy answer key for the puzzles and activities.

Indeed, there are many seasons to celebrate, and we want to make it easy for you and your students to enjoy them all!

Sincerely,

Ann

Ann Richmond Fisher

August

Get ready for an awesome August! Here is a fresh assortment of bulletin boards, teacher helps and curriculum reproducible pages to see you through many of the special days in August.

We've chosen six special themes: back-to-school, fairs, vision and learning month, watermelon, International Children's Day and National Aviation Day. For some of these themes you will find bulletin boards, parent letters and resource lists. For others you might see a song, a student game idea or an action poem. For all of the units you will have appealing reproducibles that cover important back-to-school skills. Most skill sheets are for math or language, but we've also included some pages for science, social studies and general thinking skills.

Pick the themes you are most interested in and select activities and worksheets that are on an appropriate level for your students. You will be able to use many ideas in each unit even though some individual pages may be too difficult or too easy for your particular class. You can copy the reproducible pages directly from the book. The bulletin board patterns, stationery and other items are included on the CD and numbered for easy reference.

Students will "Liftoff for Learning!" On these pages you'll find a bulletin board idea, complete with patterns. There are several beginning-of-the-year reproducibles that help students brush up on skills like counting, beginning sounds, handwriting and alphabetical order. We've even included name tags and bookmarks.

Fairs are the feature of the second section. Helpful suggestions are included for holding your own classroom fair, and under the guise of fun and games, we've covered more important math and language skills. You won't want to miss the list of resource books at the end of this portion.

Children's Vision and Learning Month is the third section. This part includes another engaging bulletin board and many reproducibles that require students to focus on visual detail. We've also included two science investigations.

Most kids love watermelon, but do yours love watermelon words? Here's a way to find out! Post our sign on a classroom wall and ask students to contribute words spelled using only the letters in *watermelon* and watch your wall fill up. After story writing, counting and more, be sure to celebrate with slices of real watermelon.

International Children's Day and National Aviation Day round out the special themes. While these are observed on specific August dates, the pages may be used at any time throughout the month (or even later if you like).

Don't forget all the great clip art on the CD. It promises to make for a truly awesome August in your classroom!

Welcome Back!

We all know that it's important to get off to a good start with each new group of students, and in this section you'll find lots of ideas right at your fingertips.

Welcome your students back to school with a bright new bulletin board. See pages 9-12 for a display idea, patterns and quick-to-cut borders. You'll find the reproducibles on pages 15-22 are perfect for the first few days of school. A stationery page, craft project and reproducible name tags and bookmarks are also included on the pages in this section.

Here are some additional ideas to help students get acquainted and begin the year with a big boost of confidence:

- Play a beanbag toss game to help students get acquainted with each other. Start the game yourself by saying, "This bag is for Jana," then toss it to Jana. Ask her to call out someone's name and toss the bag to him.

- Have each child complete something the very first day of school that he can take home to share with his family. One idea is to copy a star on page 11 so that each child has one. Ask each student to write the words, *I am a star!* on the front of the shape and then write his name on the back. Allow the students time to decorate the front with markers, crayons or glitter. It makes a great take-home souvenir for the first day of school.

- Make sure each child feels secure with his own "space" in the classroom. Use the name tags from page 23 to label desks and/or shelf space for each student.

- Create another bulletin board entitled, "Helping Hands." Feature a large octopus with eight out-stretched arms labeled with eight different classroom jobs. Under each arm, post the name of a different student each week. Or instead of the octopus, simply have each student trace his hand and label it with his name. Tack each handprint under the appropriate job listed at the top of the bulletin board. List lots of classroom jobs to include as many children as possible.

- Before students arrive, think ahead about many different ways to praise them throughout the school year. Make a lengthy list of phrases and tape it inside your grade book or plan book where you will see it often. Such phrases include, "I like the way you think"; "You have what it takes for this job"; "Whenever I need a smile, I think of you"; "That's remarkable!"; "You are incredible"; "Zowie!"; "What an imagination!"; "You're on the right track"; "Impressive"; and so on.

- Ask students to complete a brief biography collage to share with the class. Present each child with a square of colored paper, and ask her to fill it with pictures cut from magazines or drawings, letters or words of her own. Then give each student time to share his collage with the class, explaining why each item appears on it. Post all of squares in a "patchwork quilt" on a classroom wall.

Back-to-School

Write with a marker or cut out construction paper letters that spell *We're Blasting Off to a Great Start!* See the patterns on pages 10-11 and also on the CD. Use pieces of streamers or any other strips of paper for the rocket's "tail." Have each student cut out and label a star with his name.

10

Border Patterns

Back-to-School News

Back-to-School

Liftoff for Learning!

Let's liftoff for learning.
Let's get a good start.
We'll all work together
And I'll do my part.

We'll explore new words
And numbers and facts.
We'll read and write
And learn to the MAX!

It's time to get started.
It's time we've begun.
Join in the countdown:
Five, four, three, two, one—

BLAST OFF!

Instructions

Give each student his own copy of the poem so that he can follow along while you read it aloud. Introduce some of the longer words on the chalkboard such as *liftoff, together, explore* and *countdown.* Encourage the students to say as much of the poem as possible with you while you read it several more times.

- Talk about the rhyming words in the poem. How many pairs can your students identify? Can they think of more words that rhyme with each pair?
- Count backwards. In this poem, students count backwards from five. Can they do it from 10 or 20?

Name _____

Star Search

It's time to liftoff for learning and start counting!
Write the missing numbers inside the empty stars.

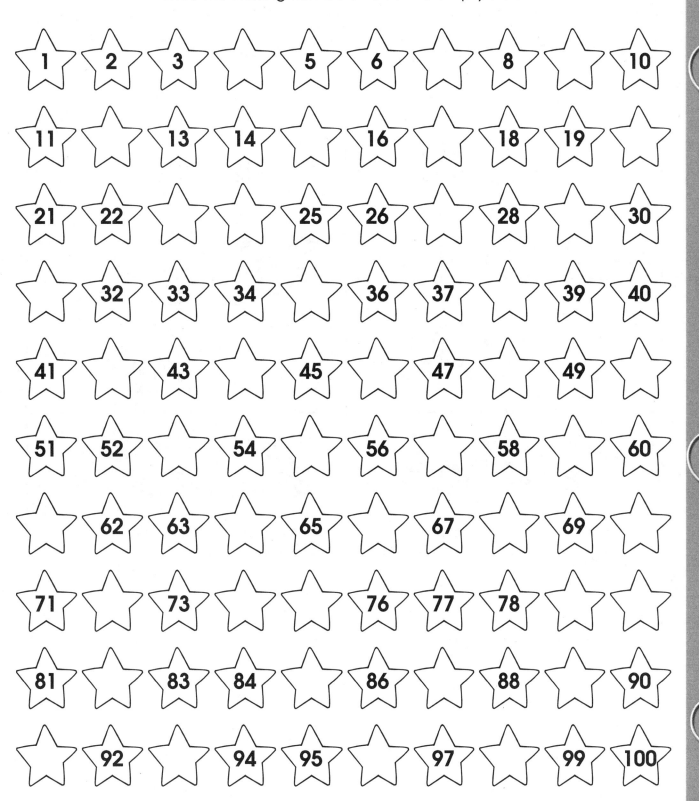

Comparing sets

School Supplies

Circle the set with the most in each box.

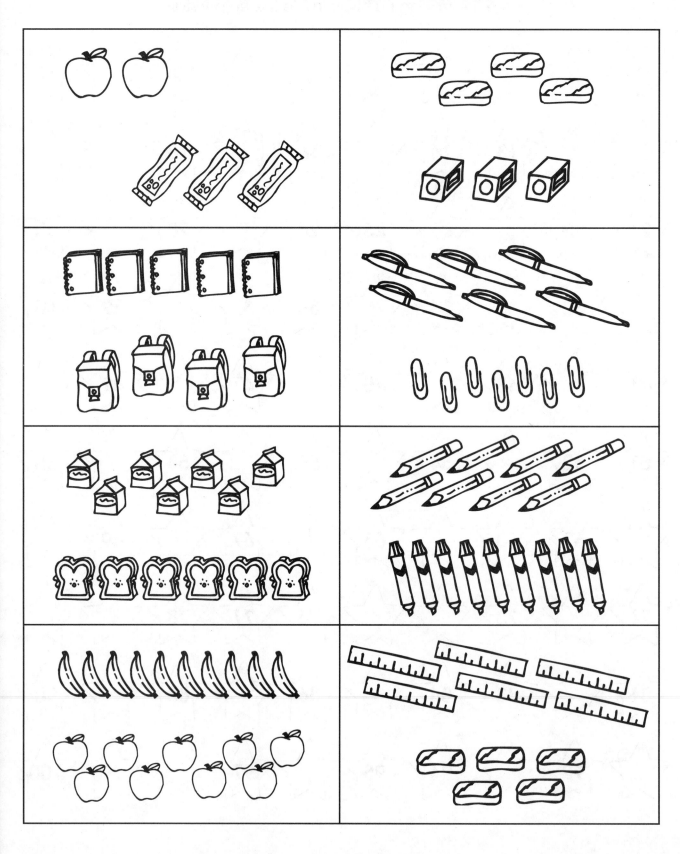

Addition with two-digit numerals

Race Pace

Which alien will win the race? Add the numbers in each lane. The runner with the highest score wins! Write the total for each runner, and circle the winner.

25	40	8	38
12	15	23	20
9	6	17	11
31	21	30	16
16	18	12	7

Totals: _____ _____ _____ _____

Finish Line

Name _____

Patterning with shapes
Shipshape

Get this page into shipshape order by drawing the shape that comes next in each line.

1.    _____

2.   _____

3.   _____

4.   _____

5.   _____

6. _____

7.  _____

Name _____

Back-to-School Names

Write your name here:

_____
- -
_____

Write your teacher's name here:

_____
- -
_____

Write the names of two girls
in your class here:

_____
- -
_____
_____
- -
_____

Write the names of two boys
in your class here:

_____
- -
_____
_____
- -
_____

Now write a sentence about one of the people named above.

_____
- -
_____
_____
- -
_____

Liftoff Letters

Write the first letter of each word in the blank.

___ ocket

___ lag

___ stronaut

___ un

___ elmet

___ ook

___ oot

___ eacher

___ oon

Name _____

Back-to-School Path

Help Amy's family get back to school. Look at the names of the places they will pass.
Number the places in ABC order. Then follow the path from 1 to 8.

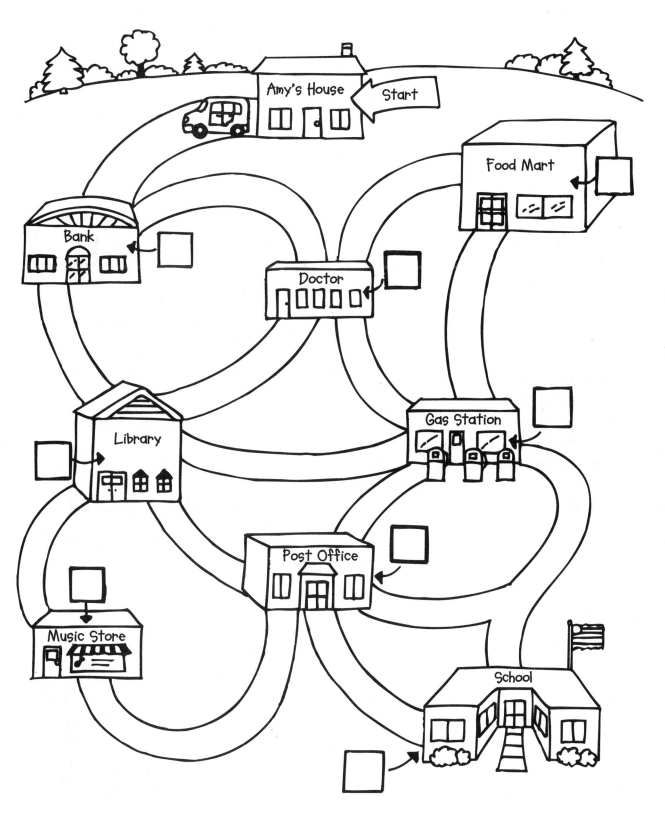

Name _____

Craft project
Pencil Pockets

Encourage your new students to get organized and settled into their desks.
Here's a simple, fun project they can do right away.

Supplies
- 8$\frac{1}{2}$" x 11" piece of paper for each student
- markers or crayons
- tape

Instructions

1. Turn the paper so that the long sides are on the top and bottom.

2. Make a fold along the top edge of the paper, about 1$\frac{1}{2}$" down.

3. Make two vertical folds, dividing the paper into thirds.

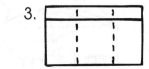

4. Be sure the top fold is facing forward. Then place the first and third sections to the back and tuck one under the other to form a flattened tube.

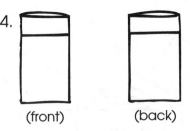

(front)   (back)

5. Now fold the tube in half. Tuck the bottom half into the flap on top to form a pocket.

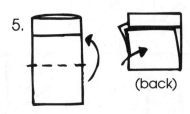

(back)

6. Decorate.

7. Tape to the side or front of the desk and use as a pencil holder.

Bookmarks & Name Tags

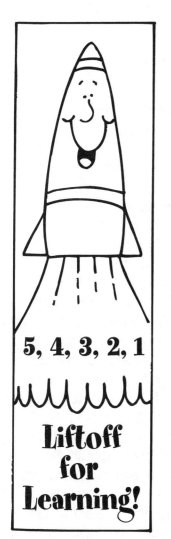

5, 4, 3, 2, 1

Liftoff for Learning!

Be a Super Star Reader!

My Name is

Reach the Stars with Books

Name

Come to the Fair!

Fairs mean fun! At least a dozen states, including California, Illinois, Michigan, New York and Ohio, hold their state fairs in the month of August. Take advantage of this special time by engaging your students in some great learning experiences. Here are some suggestions:

• Talk about the exhibits at fairs. Many students may think only of carnival rides and midway foods when they think of a fair. But to many people, the annual fair is a time to exhibit skills and projects on which they've spent an entire year. If any of your students have ever entered a project in a fair, ask them to tell the class about it. What did they make? How did they make it? How much time did they put into it? Have they ever raised animals to take to the fair? Did they receive a prize? Consider having a 4-H leader come and speak to the class.

• Some types of exhibits typically found at fairs: livestock, garden flowers and houseplants, cooking and baking, poultry, art projects, rabbits, sewing and knitting projects, electrical projects, homegrown fruits and vegetables, woodworking projects, photography, safety demonstrations, home canning and many more!

• Talk about other components of fairs, such as grandstand shows and entertainment, animal acts, carnival rides, commercial exhibits, fun foods and chance games.

• Set up your own classroom fair. Visiting a state fair may not be practical for a variety of reasons. But your class can put on its own fair! As a class, decide what you would like to have in your fair. Some blend of exhibits, acts, games and treats might be good. Choose a date far enough in advance to give your students time to prepare their exhibits. A sample parent letter is shown on page 25 that will help you communicate with parents about your special day. Plan your games and supplies needed for each (such as balloons, string, little prizes, etc.). List the types and quantities of food (including plates, napkins and spoons) you will need. In the letter, ask parents to help supply these items. Food ideas could include hot pretzels, finger gelatin, popcorn, lemonade, ice cream and cookies. Also list all the jobs that need to be done on the day of the fair, and make sure each student gets at least one task.

• Even if you decide not to hold a classroom fair, be sure to use the activities on pages 26-32 for lots of learning fun!

Clay Creations

Date: _____

Dear Parents/Caregivers,

Many states hold their annual fairs during the month of August. Our class wants to have one, too! We are planning to hold our classroom fair on

_____.

Before we hold our fair, we have a lot of work to do! First of all, I'd like each student to make a special exhibit to bring to our fair. If possible, this should be an item that he or she makes at home and brings to school the day of the fair. We have talked about many different ideas at school. Some ideas include: homemade cookies or bread; vegetables or flowers grown in your garden; a drawing, painting or poster; a craft item; a homemade booklet; an original story; etc. If you're not sure about a certain exhibit, please send in a note with your questions, and I'll get right back to you.

Secondly, we'd like to plan some activities and entertainment for our fair day. If you or your child are willing and able to share a musical number, a magic trick or short skit, please let me know.

Finally, we are also organizing games and treats for everyone who comes to our fair. We have made a list of all the supplies we'll need and are asking each family to supply one item. Could your family please help by providing _____? If this is not possible, just let me know.

Feel free to phone or write with any questions. In the meantime, please plan to attend our classroom fair! It will mean a lot to the whole class, and especially to your child!

Thanks,

_____

Counting by twos
Chickens on Parade!

These chickens are parading in front of the judges. Each pair hopes to win the blue ribbon. Count by twos to find out how many chickens are here. Write the numbers in the boxes.

There are _____ chickens in all.

Now vote for your favorite chickens. Draw a ring around the pair you like best.

Map skills

Come See the Fair!

Look at this map of the fair. Then answer the questions on the next page.

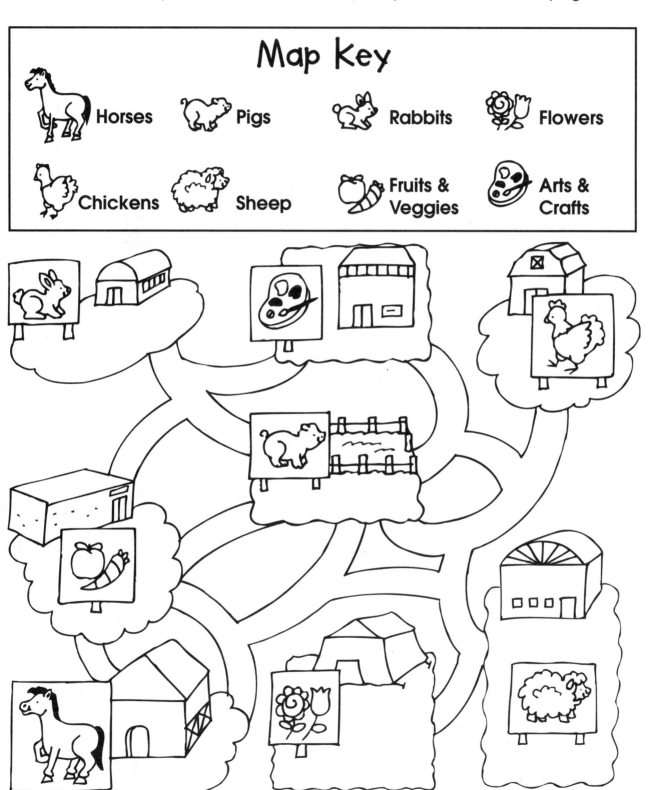

Map skills
Come See the Fair!

Write *yes* or *no*.

1. Can you see a chicken at the fair? _____

2. Can you see a zebra at the fair? _____

3. Can you see flowers at the fair? _____

4. Draw a △ to show where you can see carrots.

5. Draw a ○ to show where you can see roses.

6. Draw a ☐ to show where you can see lambs.

7. Draw a 2 to show where you can see animals with two legs.

8. Draw an ✗ to show where you can see paintings.

9. Write the name of the place you would most like to visit.

_____

Addition and subtraction
Veggie Math

Many people grow terrific vegetables and bring them to the fair to earn prizes.
Some are shown here. Count the vegetables in each box.
Then add or subtract and write the answer in the blank.

___

+___

=___ beans

___

+___

=___ carrots

___

+___

=___ tomatoes

___

+___

=___ peas

___

+___

=___ radishes

___

+___

=___ potatoes

Identifying odd numbers
Just for Fun

There are a lot of fun people to see at the fair. You'll find someone special if you carefully color in the spaces with odd numbers.

Short vowel sounds
Missing Letters

Look at all the things at the fair! Say each word and try to figure out which vowel is missing. Write the letter in the blank.

qu__lt

j___dge

s___nflower

p___g

c___lf

h__n

ch___cks

pr___tzel

___pples

tract__r

Name _____

Long and short vowel words

Ferris Wheel Words

Do you like to ride the Ferris wheel? These riders do! Look carefully at the letters around the wheel. Read the letters clockwise first, following the arrow. Write all the words you find that have long vowel sounds. Then stop at the star and read the letters backwards and write down the short vowel words that you find.

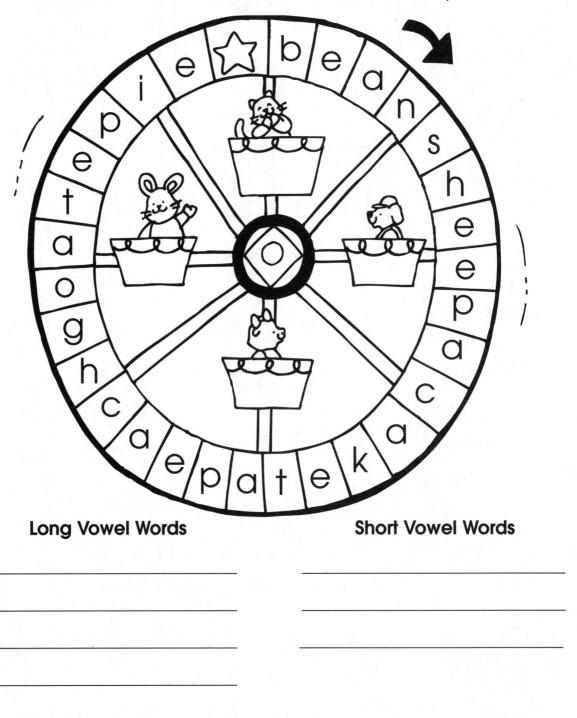

Long Vowel Words

_____

_____

_____

_____

_____

Short Vowel Words

_____

_____

_____

_____

TLC10383 Copyright © Teaching & Learning Company, Carthage, IL 62321-0010

Resources

Angelina at the Fair by Katharine Holabird. Pleasant Co. Publishing, 2000.

County Fair by Laura Ingalls Wilder. HarperCollins, 1998.

Corgiville Fair by Tash Tudor. Little, Brown, and Co, 1998.

A Day at the Fair by Patricia Hall. Simon & Schuster, 2000.

Going to the Fair by Sheryl McFarlane, Orca Book Pub., 1996.

Minerva Louise at the Fair by Janet Morgan Stoeke. Penguin Putnam Books for Young Readers, 2000.

Night at the Fair by Donald Crews. Greenwillow Books, 1998.

The Ox-Cart Man by Donald Hall. Viking Children's Books, 1979.

The Pumpkin Fair by Eileen Christelow and Eve Bunting. Houghton Mifflin, 2001.

Songs of Shiprock Fair by Luci Tapahonso. Kiva Pub., 1999.

A Week at the Fair: A Country Celebration by Patricia Harrison Easton. Millbrook Press, 1995.

Children's Vision and Learning Month

August is Children's Vision and Learning Month, and we all know that good vision is important for learning. Hopefully, all your students have had recent eye exams and have corrective lenses, if necessary. But just because kids are capable of seeing well does not ensure that they will. All students can benefit from activities that require them to look carefully to note details, to copy shapes, to sort and classify and even to use a magnifying glass to observe the finer points of many objects. Use the pages in this unit to get your students looking closely to learn.

Here are some fun classroom activities to use anytime to get your students to look and learn.

- "I'm Thinking of Something . . . ": Choose one object in your classroom and note its details. Then say to the class, "I'm thinking of something in this room that's small, green, with hard parts and soft parts. What is it?" The student who comes up with the correct answer (classroom pet turtle) gets to choose the next object to describe.

- Collect a lot of things to sort. Buttons, seeds, old greeting cards and kitchen utensils are just a few possibilities. Ask students to work in pairs to decide how they should be sorted. For example, buttons could be sorted by color, size or the number of holes they have. Then ask students to find a different way to sort the same objects.

- Play a memory game. Show the entire class (or a small group of students) a picture from a magazine or newspaper. Allow them to study it for one to two minutes. Then ask a series of questions.

- Ask students to notice what they pass on the way to school. Each morning select a different student to tell about an interesting detail she noticed.

- Play Detective Game. Ask for a volunteer to come to the front of the room. The other students should notice details about this classmate. He then leaves the room (with you) very briefly and changes one thing about his appearance. For example, he could untie one shoe, or rebutton his shirt incorrectly. Then he reappears in front of the class. The winner is the detective who first notices what is different.

- "Detective" Variation: This game can also be done with objects on a desk (to save any student from being uncomfortable from being under scrutiny). Arrange many items on a desk and ask all the students to walk around it, paying close attention to details. Then ask everyone to close their eyes. Change one thing (remove it, put it in a different place, turn it upside down, etc.). The winner is the detective who first notices what is different.

Also use the reproducibles on the remaining pages in this unit for individual work, as well as activities from other sources that work on eye-hand coordination.

Note: For the science investigations on pages 42-43, you will need to have two different types of bean seeds for each student, as well as the other items listed.

Children's Vision and Learning Month

Use the patterns on pages 36-37 (also on the CD) or add interesting items of your own from nature.

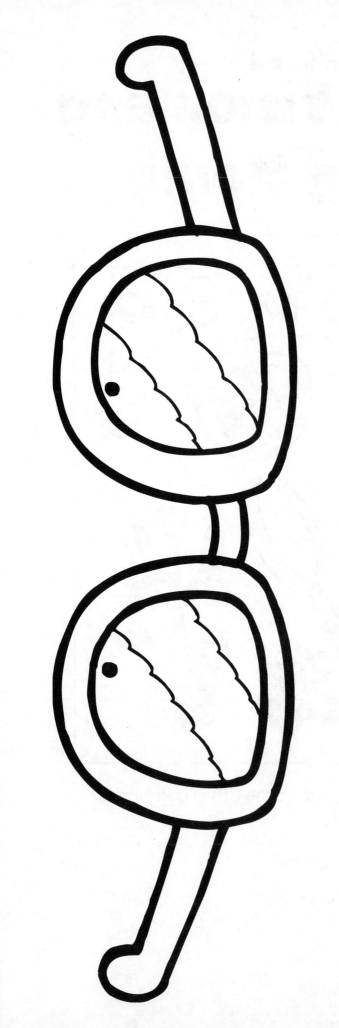

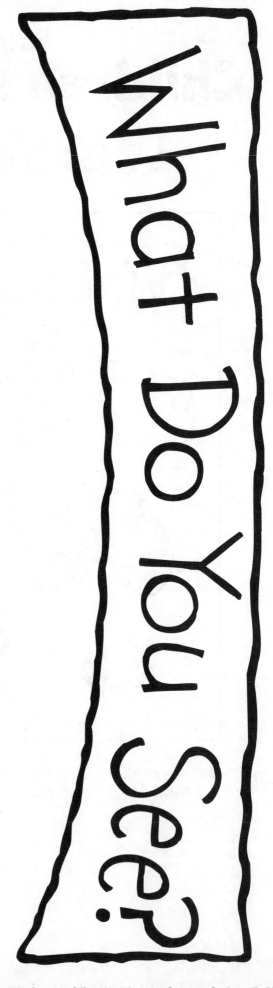

Noting and reproducing visual details

What's in the Attic?

Grandmother found a lot of things in her attic. What items in the top picture are missing in the bottom picture? Circle them in the top picture, then draw them into the bottom picture.

Using coordinates, visual matching

Match Point

Find the matching symbol in the chart. Then write its coordinates in the blank.
Give the letter first and then the number. The first one is done for you.

Name _____

Card game—visual analysis, noting attributes

Flower Power

These flowers may be different in four ways. Ask these questions about each one:
❀ Does the flower have 4 or 5 petals?   ❀ Does it have a straight stem?
❀ Does the flower have 1 or 2 leaves?   ❀ Does it have a dot in the center?

Cut out the cards and mix them up.
Then place them side by side so that each new card changes in only one way.

Name _____

What's the Next Word?

Look carefully at the first three words in each line. Then think carefully about which word should come next. Circle it and write it in the blank space.

1. pat   pet   pit   **pot**   or   **top**   _____

2. ace   bag   can   **fry**   or   **dog**   _____

3. at   pat   part   **cart** or   **party**   _____

4. cub   cube   tub   **tube** or   **rub**   _____

5. give   gave   given   **take** or   **giving**   _____

6. inch   foot   yard   **grass** or   **mile**   _____

7. care   pair   share   **fair** or   **team**   _____

8. foot   lip   arm   **coat** or   **leg**   _____

9. paint   pain   pin   **up**   or   **in**   _____

10. many   few   all   **none** or   **this**   _____

Name _____

What's in a Seed?

For this activity you will need two bean seeds,
a magnifying glass, a ruler, a plastic cup, a pencil and paper.

1. Study the seeds with the special lens. Notice how they look and feel.

2. Measure the seeds and record their sizes in a chart like this:

3. Fill the plastic cup about half full of water. Place the seeds in the water and leave them there overnight.

4. Observe the seeds again.

5. Measure the size of the seeds after soaking and record their sizes in the chart.

6. Carefully peel away the outside of one seed. Look at this outside part with the magnifying glass.

7. Separate the two halves of each bean seed.

8. Using the special lens, find the tiny plant in the seed. Make a drawing below.

	Size (mm)	
	before soaking	after soaking
1		
2		

Drawing of tiny plant inside seed

Answer these questions with your classmates:
1. How did the seeds change when they were soaked?
2. How would you describe the outside of the bean seed before it was soaked? After it was soaked?
3. Where in the seed was the tiny plant?

Name _____

Teacher: You will need to start nine bean seedlings for each student or group of students prior to this investigation.

Science investigation
Learn About Light

For this activity you will need three paper cups, nine bean (or flower) seedlings, potting soil, labels, water, two tall boxes or paper sacks, a pencil and paper.

1. Label each cup with one of these words: *Light, No Light, Some Light.*

2. Label the tall boxes or sacks with: *Some Light, No Light.*

3. Use the potting soil to plant three seedlings in each cup. Add equal amounts of water to each cup so the soil is moist.

4. Place the box labeled *No Light* over the cup with the same label. Place the cups labeled *Light* and *Some Light* near a window.

5. Every day at noon place the box labeled *Some Light* over the cup with the same label. Remove the box every morning.

6. Check the soil in each cup every two days. Add equal amounts of water to each cup if needed.

7. After one week, observe the seedlings in each cup. Do you notice any changes? Write or draw the differences between the plants in the three cups.

8. After a second week, observe and record any changes as well.

9. What conclusions can you draw from your observations?

Name _____

Animal Count

To count things in order, we use order words, or ordinal numbers.
The ordinal number each bear is holding tells the bear's place in line.

first   second   third   fourth   fifth   sixth   seventh   eighth   ninth   tenth

Use your good vision to look carefully at each ordinal number word. Then count the animals in each row and circle the correct one.

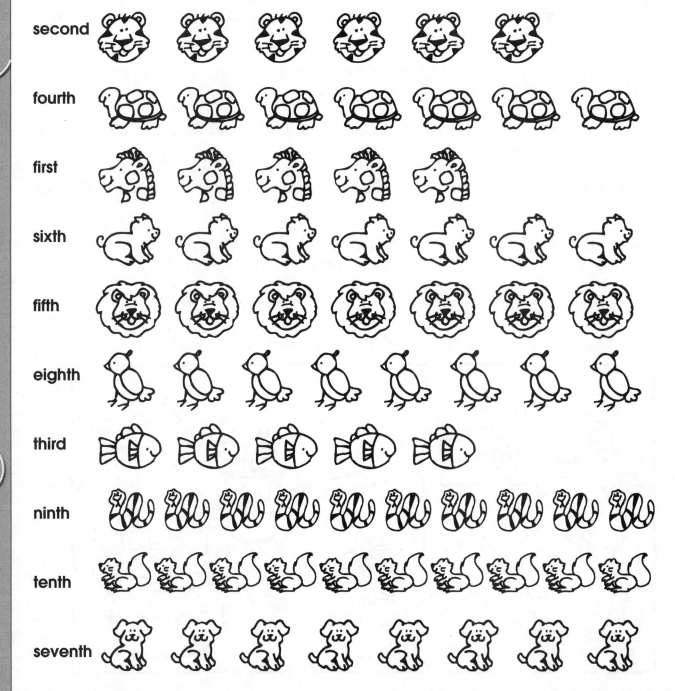

second

fourth

first

sixth

fifth

eighth

third

ninth

tenth

seventh

It's Watermelon Time!

August is the best month for homegrown watermelons, and Watermelon Festivals are held in Hope, Arkansas, and Rush Springs, Oklahoma, every year during this month.

Start your own classroom watermelon festival with this fun language arts activity. First, post the signage on page 46 somewhere on a classroom wall. Then ask students to think of words that can be spelled using the letters in *WATERMELON*. Each time a student thinks of a new word, ask him to write it carefully on a watermelon-shaped piece of paper and add it to the classroom display. A sample pattern is below.

Next, ask students to write watermelon stories. Here are some sample story starters you may want to use for group or individual stories:

- A watermelon tastes like . . .
- I love to eat juicy watermelon because . . .
- Watermelon seeds feel like . . .
- One day I found the biggest watermelon in the world . . .
- I think watermelon would taste good with . . .

These stories can be copied into shape books, using the pattern on page 47.

Then try some of the reproducible activities that appear on pages 48-51. Finally, be sure to serve some juicy watermelon—along with plenty of napkins—as a special treat. (You may wish to notify families in advance so that students do not wear their best clothes to school that day.) Before you cut up the watermelon, ask students to try to lift it and guess its weight. Then weigh it on bathroom scales for all to see.

We Love Watermelon Words!

Shape Book Pattern

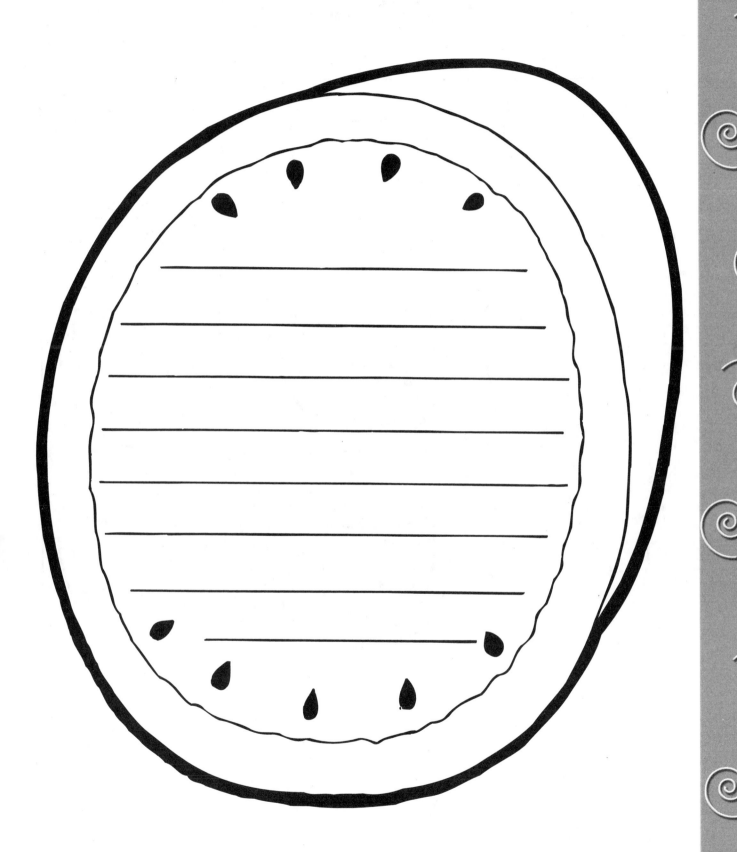

Counting and adding up to 20

Seed Count

Count the number of seeds on each slice of watermelon. Then add more seeds to each slice until the number of seeds matches the number below it.

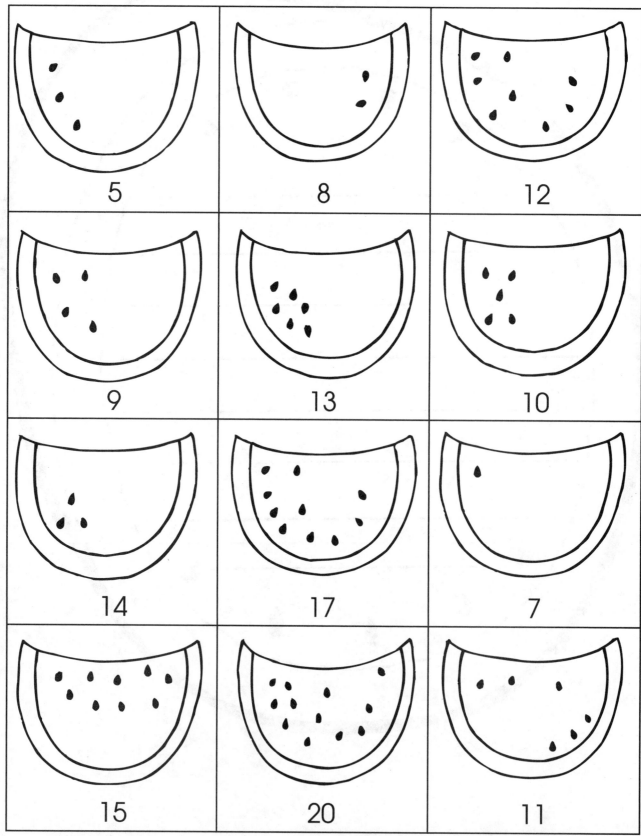

My Very Own Watermelon

Read this poem with your students. Then read it again and ask them to do the actions.

I planted a seed
And poked it into the dirt.
I packed it gently
Then wiped my hands on my shirt.

(Bend over and pretend to drop a seed.)
(Poke the floor with index finger.)
(Use both hands to pat the floor.)
(Wipe hands on shirt.)

The rain gave it water.
The sun gave it light.
Up came a small green sprout
And it grew just right.

(Wave fingers to show raindrops falling.)
(Extend arms and join hands above head to show sun.)
(Bend over and pretend to measure small plant with thumb and first finger.)

The little sprout grew bigger
And soon was a long green vine.
First with three leaves,
Then six, and then nine!

(Show with thumb and first finger a growing plant.)
(Stretch both arms out to the side.)
(Hold up three fingers.)
(Hold up six, then nine fingers.)

After some blossoms
More rain and more sun
I waited longer and then—
The first little melon had begun!

(Pretend to smell a flower.)
(Show raindrops and sun again as above.)
(Tap foot as if waiting.)
(Show a small round object with one hand.)

The melon grew bigger
Every single day,
And I began to wonder,
"How much will it weigh?"

(Use two hands to show growing size of round object.)
(Shrug both shoulders and look around questioningly.)

Finally the big day came
When we picked it from the vine
We sliced it and tasted it,
And I said,
"This is the best watermelon EVER because it's MINE!"

(Pretend to pick and lift heavy object.)
(Pretend to eat a slice.)

(Smile and point to self.)

Sequencing

Time to Grow

Number the pictures from 1 to 6 to show what comes first, second and so on.

Name _____

Melon Matchup

Watermelon is a compound word made up of the two smaller words *water* and *melon*. There are many more compound words, and you will find some of them on this page. Draw a line from a melon slice on the left to one on the right that makes a sensible compound word. Write more compound words that you know on the back of this page.

basket

sun

ground

walk

stop

milk

ball

flower

straw

grass

hopper

watch

side

grand

berry

mother

news

play

paper

shake

Name _____

Communities

We all belong to many different communities—from our family community to our world community. Look at the names of different communities. Draw a picture for each.

Family	School
Neighborhood	**City or Town**
Country	**Planet**

1. Which community contains the most people? _____

2. How many people are in your family community? _____

3. How many people are in your school community? _____

Name _____

Map It Out

This map shows the land and water that are on the Earth.
A continent is a large mass of land, and there are seven continents on the Earth.
An ocean is a large body of water. This maps shows four large oceans.

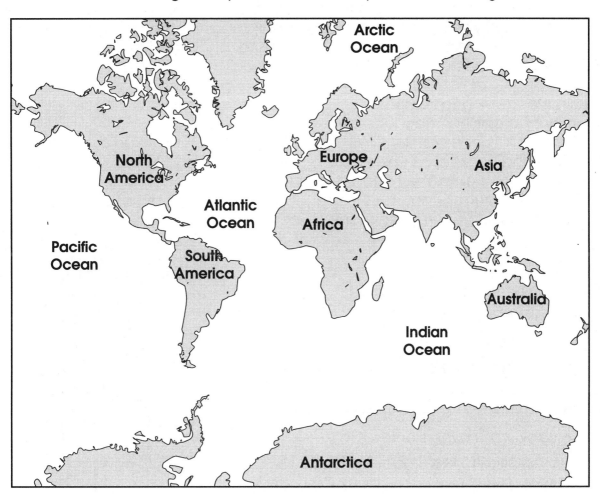

1. Find the names of the seven continents on the map and circle them.

2. Write their names here: _____ _____ _____

_____ _____ _____ _____

3. Color the land areas green. Draw a red X on the continent where you live.

4. Find the names of four oceans on the map and underline them.

5. Write the ocean names here: _____ _____

_____ _____

6. Color the water blue. Draw a black X on the ocean closest to your home.

Name _____

Can we have a title?

Read this story. Then answer the questions at the bottom.

Betsy woke up very excited. "This is the day!" she said to herself. Betsy was seven years old, and today she was taking a long airplane ride across the ocean. It would be her very first flight.

Her family was moving to Ireland because her parents had new jobs there. Betsy's family had been packing their clothes, toys and books into trunks and suitcases for many weeks. They had moved their furniture to Grandma's basement. They had said good-bye to many friends.

Betsy had been learning about children in Ireland. She learned that most of them speak English, that most kids wear uniforms to school and that summer vacation is only during July and August. She learned that Ireland is an island country which is very green and beautiful.

Even though Betsy loved to read about children in Ireland, she couldn't wait to actually meet some Irish children and make new friends of her own in her new community.

1. A good title for this story would be:

    a. Betsy's First Plane Ride

    b. Irish People

    c. Moving to Ireland

Write T in front of a true sentence. Write N if it is not true.

_____ 2. Betsy was 11 years old.

_____ 3. Betsy liked to learn about Ireland.

_____ 4. Betsy was looking forward to moving to Ireland.

_____ 5. Betsy has taken many plane rides.

_____ 6. Her family was taking their furniture with them.

_____ 7. Her family was taking clothes, books and toys to Ireland.

_____ 8. Irish children go to school in June.

Write a short story about children in a country that you would like to visit.

_____

_____

_____

_____

54

Color by number
Flag Fun

Color these flags from different countries by matching the numbers to these colors:

1 = red   2 = blue   3 = green   4 = yellow   5 = orange

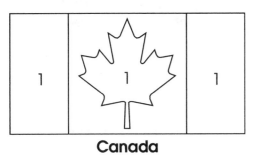

Canada

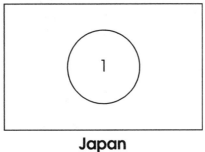

Japan

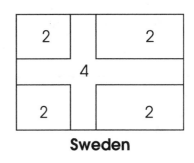

Sweden

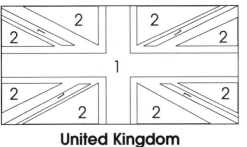

United Kingdom

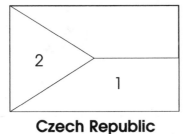

Czech Republic

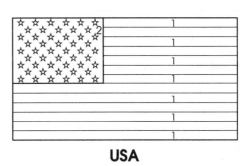

USA

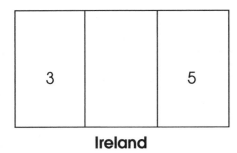

Ireland

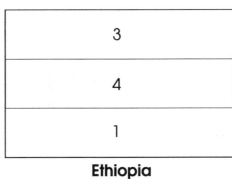

Ethiopia

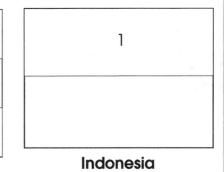

Indonesia

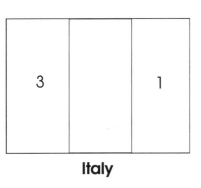

Italy

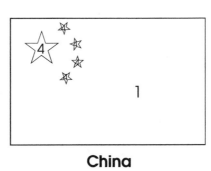

China

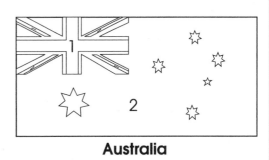

Australia

Now try to find each country on a map or globe.

Capital letters, ABC order

Capital Countries

The name of a country always begins with a capital letter.
Write these names in ABC order, and spell each country's name with a capital letter.

turkey	yemen	nigeria	libya	france	spain
iran	brazil	denmark	cuba	egypt	peru

1. _____   7. _____

2. _____   8. _____

3. _____   9. _____

4. _____   10. _____

5. _____   11. _____

6. _____   12. _____

TLC10383 Copyright © Teaching & Learning Company, Carthage, IL 62321-0010

Name _____

Flag Tags

A certain shop sells flags from many countries. The flags are priced according to the spelling of the country. First look at the chart and see that A = $1, B = $2 on through Z = $26. Then find the price for the flags listed by adding the correct numbers together.

Example: CHAD = 3 + 8 + 1 + 4 = $16   A flag from Chad sells for $16.

Before you find the prices, first try to make some predictions.
Which flag do you think will cost the most? Circle it.
Which do you think will cost the least? Underline it.

1. PERU _____	A = $1
	B = $2
	C = $3
2. INDIA _____	D = $4
	E = $5
	F = $6
3. MALI _____	G = $7
	H = $8
	I = $9
4. IRAQ _____	J = $10
	K = $11
	L = $12
5. CANADA _____	M = $13
	N = $14
	O = $15
6. NEPAL _____	P = $16
	Q = $17
	R = $18
7. PANAMA _____	S = $19
	T = $20
	U = $21
8. FIJI _____	V = $22
	W = $23
	X = $24
Were your predictions correct? _____	Y = $25
	Z = $26

National Aviation Day

August 19 is known as National Aviation Day. Orville Wright, who piloted the first self-powered flight in 1903 was born on August 19, 1871. In 1939, President Franklin Roosevelt proclaimed Orville's birthday National Aviation Day, and it has remained so ever since.

Here are some ideas of how to observe this special day with your primary grade students:

• Talk about airplane trips. Ask if any students have traveled by plane. If they have, ask them where they went and what they thought of the experience. Discuss the process of getting tickets, checking in, going through security, boarding, buckling up, etc. Be careful to listen to and talk about fears children may have regarding flying.

• If possible, visit an airport, airstrip or aviation museum.

• Invite someone from the airline industry to speak to the class. Perhaps you could locate a pilot, flight attendant, travel agent, airplane mechanic or other person to visit your class and speak about her job.

• Play a favorite memory and phonics game, "I'm going on a trip, and I'm taking a . . ." The first child says the sentence and names something that begins with an A. The second child says the sentence, adds the A answer and then adds a B answer of his own. The third child repeats both previous answers and adds a C answer. The third child's answer might be something like, "I'm going on a trip, and I'm taking an apple, a bandanna and some candy." It becomes more and more difficult to remember all the answers, but you may

choose to allow classmates to help each other. You may also want to encourage silly answers, such as an armadillo, a bison and a Christmas tree. This is a game you can play many times, especially if you rearrange students so the same ones don't always come at the end of the alphabet.

• Make some paper airplanes. Take them outside for test flights. Experiment with different weights of paper, different designs and so on.

• Role-play the process of taking a flight. Set up a check-in desk, airline seats, cockpit, control tower, etc. Talk about the different responsibilities of each job and what it's like to be a passenger.

• Try out the reproducibles on the pages that follow.

Name _____

We're Going on a Trip

Sing several rounds of this action song as you celebrate National Aviation Day!

To the tune of "The Farmer in the Dell"

First Verse

We're going on a trip,
We're going on a trip,
Hi-ho the dairy-o,
We're going on a trip.

(Action: Folding clothes, gathering toys, etc., to pack a suitcase.)

Second Verse

We're flying in a plane,
We're flying in a plane,
Hi-ho the dairy-o,
We're flying in a plane.

(Action: Arms extended, lifting and tilting as students walk around the room pretending to be airplanes.)

Third Verse

We're eating in the plane,
We're eating in the plane, . . .

(Pretend to spread a piece of bread with butter and eat it.)

Fourth Verse

We're sleeping on the plane,
We're sleeping on the plane, . . .

(Pretend to yawn and snuggle, then close eyes.)

Fifth Verse

Our trip is almost done,
Our trip is almost done, . . .

(Stretch, put on jacket, etc.)

Sixth Verse

We're climbing off the plane,
We're climbing off the plane, . . .

(Walk down a flight of stairs.)

Seventh Verse

The flying was great fun,
The flying was great fun.

(Clap.)

Students may want to omit some of these verses and make up new ones of their own.

Name _____

Skywriting

This happy skywriter is zooming around making all the ABCs with his airplane.
He has only two letters left to make. What are they?
Write them in the blanks behind the airplane.

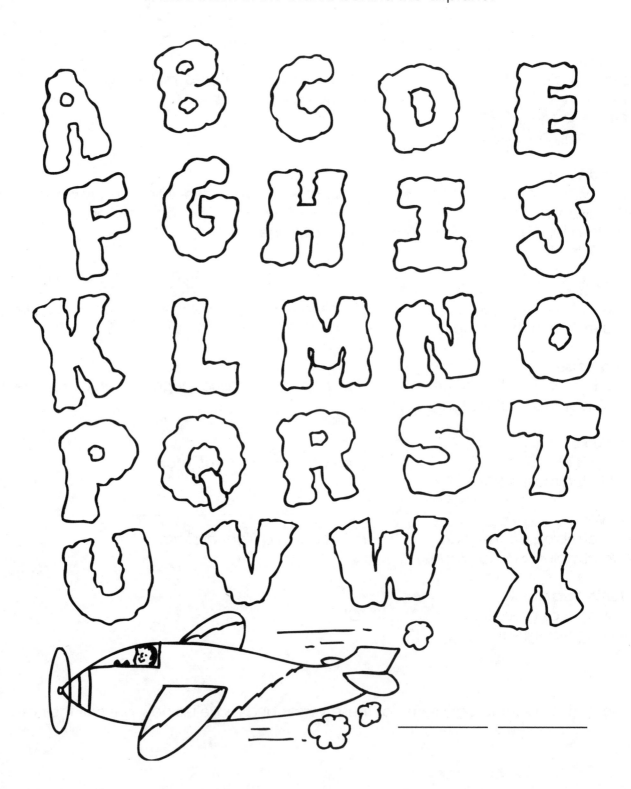

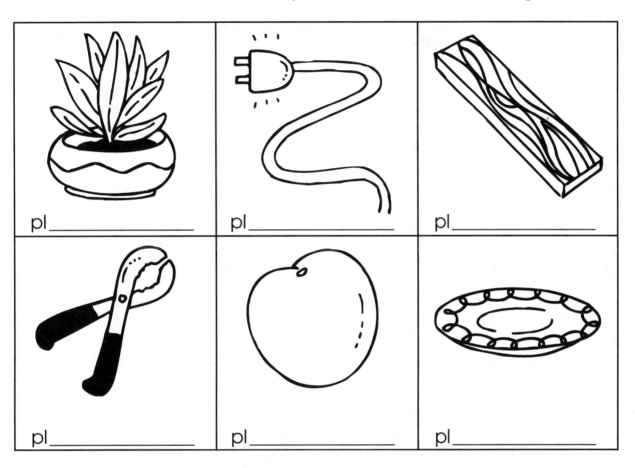

Name _____

Pl-Pl-Please Help!

These pictures show words that start with *pl*, just like the word *plane*.
Write the correct letters in each blank to finish the words.
Then find the words in the puzzle at the bottom of the page.

pl_____   pl_____   pl_____

pl_____   pl_____   pl_____

P	G	U	L	P	S
L	K	F	O	R	P
U	N	Q	E	B	L
M	A	I	X	D	A
C	L	G	M	J	N
P	P	S	W	V	T
E	T	A	L	P	H

Name _____

The Wright Brothers—Article

Listen carefully to this article about Orville and Wilbur Wright, and be ready to answer some questions together when I have finished reading it to you.

Orville Wright was born on August 19, 1871. His older brother, Wilbur was already four years old. Orville was born in Ohio, and Wilbur was born in Indiana. Their father was a minister. Later the Wrights moved to North Carolina.

Both boys were interested in mechanical things while they were still young. Sadly, Wilbur had a skating accident which handicapped him for several years. Even as young boys, the two were very interested in things that flew. They played with kites and a toy helicopter. They learned about gliders and studied how birds kept their balance in the air.

Orville was a hard worker. While he was still in high school, he built a printing press and started a weekly newspaper. The brothers were close friends, and neither of them married.

In 1892, when Orville was about 21, the brothers opened a bicycle shop. They sold new bikes and repaired old ones. Soon they were making their own bikes. Then in 1900, they built their first glider. They made 200 different model wings and tested them in a small wind tunnel. Two years later, in 1902, they built a glider that beat all records for flight!

Next, the brothers built their first powered airplane. It was called the *Flyer I*. They worked hard to build just the right engine and propeller for it. Then on December 17, 1903, with a strong wind at Kitty Hawk, North Carolina, Orville flew the plane. He kept it up in the air for 12 seconds. He had just made history! Wilbur flew the plane for the longest flight of the day which lasted 59 seconds.

In the years that followed, the Wrights built and tested new planes and engines. They made planes that were better and that would do more things. They even earned the right to build the world's first military plane.

Teacher: You may wish to read the article through a second time before asking your students the questions on page 63.

The Wright Brothers

1. What was Orville's brother's name? (Wilbur)

2. Which brother was older? (Wilbur)

3. When did the boys become interested in mechanical things? (while they were still young)

4. What kind of flying toys did they play with? (kites and a helicopter)

5. What kind of shop did the boys open when Orville was about 21 years old? (bicycle)

6. What services did they provide in their bicycle shop? (They sold new bikes, repaired old bikes and eventually made their own bikes.)

7. How do you think the bicycle shop prepared them for building their own glider? (It gave them experience in building something moving that worked, it gave them confidence to try new things, etc. Answers will vary.)

8. Orville and Wilbur built over 200 model wings and tested them before building their record-breaking glider. What does this tell you about their willingness to work? (They worked hard. They didn't give up easily. They worked until they were successful. Answers will vary.)

9. What was the name of the brothers' first powered airplane? (*Flyer I*)

10. Where did the first flight take place? (Kitty Hawk, North Carolina)

11. Which brother was the pilot for the very first flight? (Orville)

12. Which brother had the longest flight that day? (Wilbur)

13. Why do you think Wilbur and Orville kept building better planes and engines? (They wanted to excel in their work. As they had more experiences, they came up with new ideas. They enjoyed finding a better way. Answers will vary.)

Name _____

Airplane Graph

The pilots at City Airport like to keep track of how many times they fly each week.
Here is their graph. Each plane picture means one flight.
Study the graph, and then answer the questions.

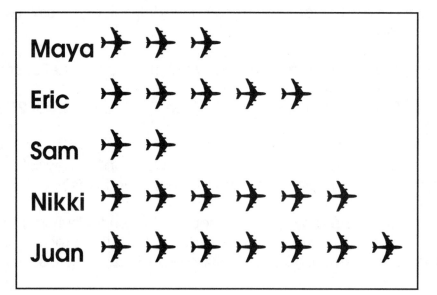

1. How many times did Nikki fly? _____

2. How many times did Eric fly? _____

3. Who flew the most times? _____

4. Who flew the fewest times? _____

5. Did Maya fly one more time than Sam?   yes   no

6. Did Eric fly two more times than Sam?   yes   no

7. Who flew three more times than Maya? _____

8. How many times did Eric and Sam fly altogether? _____

Name _____

Telling time
Flight Schedules

The City Airport's five pilots just learned at what time they fly out again.
Show the correct time on the clocks.

Maya—5:00

Eric—9:30

Sam—10:00

Nikki—12:30

Juan—3:30

Show the time that you leave for school.

Suppose that Nikki left one hour *later* than shown above. What time would that be? _____
Show it on the clock.

Suppose that Sam, left one hour *earlier* than shown above. What time would that be?

_____

Show it on the clock.

Resources

All Aboard Airplanes by Frank Evans. The Putnam Publishing Group, 1994.

The Berenstain Bears Fly-It!: Up, Up and Away by Stan and Jan Berenstain. Random House, Inc, 1996.

First Flight: The Story of Tom Tate and the Wright Brothers (I Can Read Chapter Book Series) by George Shea. HarperCollins Children's Books, 1997.

Flight by Robert Burleigh. Putnam Publishing Group, 1997.

Kids Paper Airplane Book with Poster by Ken Blackburn and Jeff Lammers. Workman Publishing, 1996.

Look Inside an Airplane by Patrizia Malfatti. Putnam Books for Young Readers, 2000.

The Magic School Bus Taking Flight: A Book About Flight by Joanna Cole and Gail Herman. Scholastic, 1997.

Plane Song by Diane Siebert. HarperCollins Publishers, 1995.

Taking Flight: The Story of the Wright Brothers by Stephen Krensky, Simon & Schuster, 2001.

Wilbur and Orville Wright: The Flight of Adventure by Louis Sabin, Troll Communications, 1997.

Wright Brothers by Mary Tucker. Teaching & Learning Company, 2002.

September

Six special themes lead the way to a spectacular September! National Honey Month, National Courtesy Month, Labor Day, Grandparents' Day, Mexican Independence Day and Elephant Appreciation Day. For some of these themes you will find bulletin boards, songs, drawing pages and resource lists. For all of the units you will have appealing reproducibles that cover important back-to-school skills. Most skill sheets are for math or language, but we've also included pages for science, social studies and general thinking skills. Don't miss the final section of the month which contains a bulletin board, bookmarks and other resources that are good for the entire month. A helpful answer key is found at the end of the book.

You can copy the reproducible pages and patterns directly from the book. The bulletin board patterns, stationery and other items are included on the CD and numbered for easy reference.

Look for naturally sweet learning activities for National Honey Month. On pages 68-77 you'll find honey facts, recipes and reproducibles. A factual article focuses on science and reading comprehension; long vowel sounds, sequencing and subtraction are also covered.

Promote good manners during National Courtesy Month. Included on pages 78-88 are a bulletin board, a listening lesson and reproducibles for important math and language skills. Expect students to work on writing simple sentences, identifying nouns, completing a bar graph and more.

Learn about community workers and parents' jobs for Labor Day. This part includes another bulletin board and ideas for parent involvement. Some of the curriculum skills covered are beginning consonants, counting by 10s, money and tools.

The upbeat Grandparents' Day unit includes a great greeting card and suggestions for a Grandparents' Open House.

A brief unit on Mexican Independence Day includes a map of the country and work with Spanish words.

Perhaps the most unique (and fun!) unit is the one for Elephant Appreciation Day on pages 113-121. Honor these incredible creatures while you sneak in some great kids' books, a factual article, sentence skills, animal classification and more.

Finally, don't forget all the great clip art on the CD. It promises to make for a truly spectacular September in your classroom!

National Honey Month

September is National Honey Month, in honor of beekeepers and honeybees! Did you know that in the U.S.A., there are more than 200,000 beekeepers, and over 2.6 million colonies of honeybees? Together they produce more than 200 million pounds of honey each year. Take advantage of this special month by teaching your students about how bees work and how honey is made.

Honey Facts

- Bees are the only insects that make food for people.

- Bees may travel up to 55,000 miles and visit more than two million flowers to find enough nectar to make just one pound of honey!

- A worker honeybee makes only $1/12$ of a teaspoon of honey in her lifetime.

- Bees make honey, but they also do another very important job. They pollinate a variety of fruits, vegetables and other crops.

- About one-third of the human diet comes from pollinated plants, and honeybees do about 80% of this pollination.

- Honey is made mostly of fructose, glucose and water.

- The color and flavor of honey depends on the flowers from which the nectar is gathered.

- We are most familiar with liquid honey. It is extracted from the honeycomb by straining or using centrifugal force.

- Whipped honey is also available as a spread. It is honey that has crystallized under controlled conditions.

- Comb honey comes as it was produced by bees–in the bee's wax comb. You can purchase it in some stores or from beekeepers. The comb and honey are both edible!

- A place where several bee colonies are kept is called an apiary.

Use the article and questions on page 73 to teach your students more about bees and honey. Check out the great story and nature books and on page 77 as well. No section on National Honey Month would be complete without recipes! A few simple ones are included on the next two pages. Plan ahead and ask parents to help "cook" or supply ingredients.

You can purchase an educational video and teacher's guide from the National Honey Board, BBMAT, 390 Langley St., Longmont, CO 80501. You may also visit their web site for more free information and recipes at www.honey.com.

Honey Recipes

Honey Crisp Cookies

Makes about 30.

1/2 cup powdered sugar
1/2 cup honey
1/2 cup peanut butter
1 1/2 cups crisp rice cereal
1/2 cup raisins
1/2 cup multicolored candy sprinkles

Cover a plate or cookie sheet with waxed paper. Combine powdered sugar, honey and peanut butter in a medium bowl. Mix well. Stir in cereal and raisins. Using clean hands, shape mixture into 1" balls. Roll in sprinkles and place on cookie sheet. Refrigerate for one hour or until cookies feel firm. Serve or store in tightly covered container in refrigerator.

Bananas on a Stick

This recipe makes eight servings. Adjust amounts according to the number of students in your class.

4 ripe bananas, cut in half
1/2 cup honey
8 wooden craft sticks
1 1/3 cups graham cracker crumbs (Buy crumbs already prepared, or use about 18 square crackers. Place in a gallon-sized resealable plastic bag and crush with a rolling pin until fine.)

Place each banana half on a stick. Hold banana over a plate to catch drips. Drizzle honey over banana, coating all sides. (Squirt it slowly from a bottle, or use a spoon.) Roll banana in graham cracker crumbs. Press with clean fingertips to help them stick. Place on cookie sheet lined with waxed paper. Serve at once.

Edible Honey Dough

You may want to make one batch for every three to four students.

1 cup peanut butter
1 cup honey
2 cups powdered milk

Wash your hands. Mix the three ingredients in a bowl. Add more milk powder if the dough is too sticky. Form the dough into the letters in your name or into other shapes of your choice. Eat your creation.

Fruitti-Tutti Pops

Makes 12 servings.

3 cups of any fresh or canned fruit, cut into small pieces
2 1/4 cups water
3/4 cup honey
12 3-oz. disposable cups
12 wooden craft sticks

Place 1/4 cup of fruit in each cup. In a pitcher, whisk together honey and water until well blended. Pour even amounts of mixture into the 12 cups. Place in freezer until partially frozen, or about an hour. Place one stick in each cup. Freeze until firm. Serve.

Note

Most pediatricians do not recommend giving honey to children under one year because of the possibility that it may contain spores that can cause illness in infants. Caution is advised when sharing these recipes with families. As always, be aware of any peanut or other food allergies your students may have.

Honey-Sweetened Homemade Ice Cream

1 pint real cream (as for whipping)
1/3 cup honey
1 tsp. vanilla
1 pinch of table salt
large aluminum can with plastic lid
        (such as a coffee can)
large pail
wooden spoon with a hole in it
crushed ice cubes
rock salt or box of table salt

Pour cream, honey, vanilla and the pinch of salt into aluminum can and mix well. Poke a hole large enough for spoon handle in the plastic lid of the aluminum can. Push the spoon handle through the hole and place the lid on the can. Fill the bottom of the bucket with ice. Set the cream mixture on top of the ice. Pour a layer of salt on the ice. Layer more ice and salt until it reaches the top of the aluminum can. Let stand for 5 minutes. Twirl the wooden spoon many times. (Students can take turns with this!) Turn the entire can periodically. As the ice melts, add more layers of ice and salt. After 15-20 minutes, the spoon will be difficult to twirl. Check the ice cream. If it's too soft, continue to stir and add ice. When the ice cream is just the way you want it, remove from the bucket and can and serve. Enjoy!

Honey Parfaits

sliced bananas, strawberries or peaches
honey
plain yogurt
granola or other crunchy cereal
9- or 12-oz. plastic cups

Place a layer of fruit in bottom of cup. Drizzle with a tablespoon of honey. Add a layer of yogurt and cereal. Top with more sliced fruit and another tablespoon of honey.

Other Easy Honey Treats

- Toast whole wheat bread or an English muffin. Spread with cream cheese and drizzle with honey.

- Mix 1/2 cup peanut butter with 1/4 cup of honey. Use as a dip for apple or pear slices, carrot and celery sticks or even hot chicken nuggets. Delicious!

- Instead of chocolate syrup, use a squirt of honey on top of ice cream.

Visual discrimination
Hive Homes

Which bee flew out of each hive? Follow their trails and find out.
Write the correct number next to each bee.

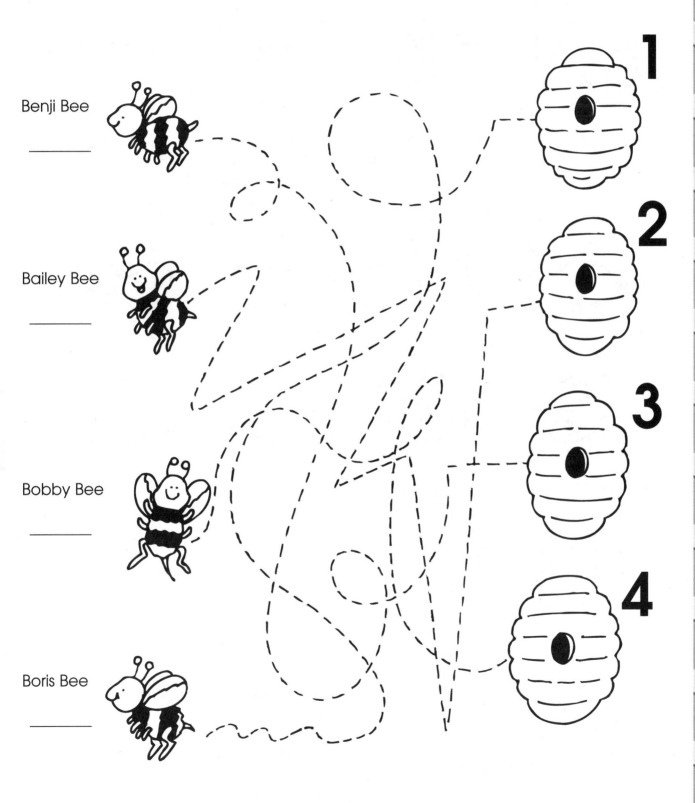

Benji Bee

_____

Bailey Bee

_____

Bobby Bee

_____

Boris Bee

_____

Name _____

Long vowel sounds
Bee-Long!

The word *bee* contains the long *e* sound. Here are other words with long vowel sounds:

grapes

kite

bone

mule

Read the word written on each bee. If it is a long vowel sound, color the bee yellow.
If it is not a long vowel sound, color the bee orange.
Draw a line to connect all the long vowel bees.

 hole

 she

 hot

 pin

 light

 comb

 sheep

 cube

 sun

 me

 late

 use

 fine

 sat

 bake

 home

Name _____

Worker Bees

Honeybees live in large groups called colonies. Each colony contains one queen bee, some drone bees and many worker bees. There are more worker bees than drones.

The worker bees have a lot to do! They build the nest, or hive, and care for the very young bees. They build the nest from wax made in their bodies. The nest is made of six-side cells and is called a comb. Some of the cells are used for keeping the young, developing bees. Other cells are used to store honey.

Worker bees leave the hive to gather nectar, pollen and water. Nectar is a liquid. Pollen is a powder. Both are made by flowers. The workers use the nectar, pollen and water to make honey. They also feed the other bees and clean the comb. Sometimes they have to keep other animals and people away from their hive by using their stingers. If the nest becomes too hot, they cool it off by fanning their wings.

1. The main idea of the article is:

   a. Worker bees make honey.

   b. Worker bees have many jobs.

   c. Pollen and nectar are made by flowers.

2. How many queen bees live in each nest? _____

3. What is the name for a bee's nest? _____

4. How do worker bees keep the nest cool? _____

5. Where do workers find the wax for building the nest?

   a. in flowers

   b. inside the drone bees

   c. It is made in their own bodies.

6. Why do workers sometime use their stingers?

   a. because they want to keep people and animals away from their nest

   b. because their stingers get stuck

   c. because their stingers help them to make honey

Science, sequencing

Busy Bees!

Beehives are very busy places! Look at the pictures and read
the sentences that tell what the bees are doing.
Number the pictures from 1 to 6 to show the order in which the work is done.

The eggs hatch and little bees come out.

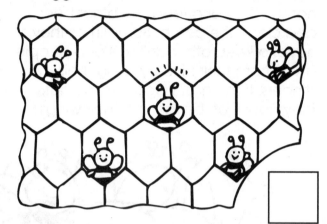

The hive becomes larger and larger.

Worker bees begin to build a nest or hive.

The worker bees gather pollen and
nectar from plants.

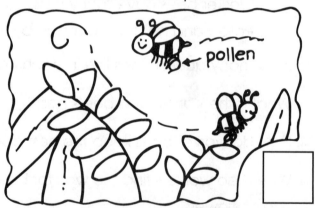

pollen

The workers bring the pollen back to the
hive to make honey and feed the young
bees and queen bee.

The queen bee lays eggs in the hive.

Name _____

Subtraction
Beehive Math

Outside each hive you'll see a lot of busy bees. Count them.
The number shows how many flew away. Cross out that many bees.
Count the ones that are left. Write the number on the line.

 − 2 = _____

 − 4 = _____

 − 5 = _____

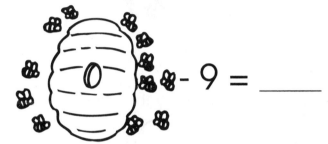 − 9 = _____

 − 7 = _____

 − 8 = _____

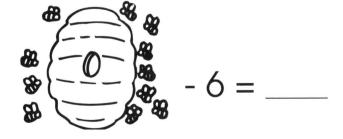 − 6 = _____

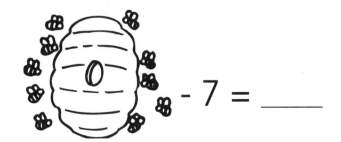 − 9 = _____

 − 6 = _____

− 7 = _____

One-half
Half-Time

$\frac{1}{2}$ of this honeycomb has been colored.

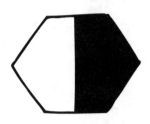

Color $\frac{1}{2}$ of this hive.

Color $\frac{1}{2}$ of this flower.

Color $\frac{1}{2}$ of this bee.

Color $\frac{1}{2}$ of this butterfly.

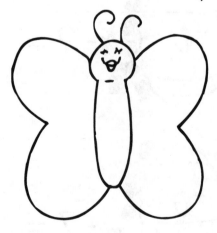

Color $\frac{1}{2}$ of this flower.

Resources

These are some recommended storybooks and nature books related to bees and honey. Books are for ages 4-8 unless otherwise indicated.

The Bear Who Didn't Like Honey by Barbara Maitland, Orchard Books, 1997.

The Bee Tree by Patricia Polacco, Putnam, 1998.

Big Honey Hunt by Stan and Jan Berenstain, Random House, 1962.

Busy, Buzzy Bee (Level 1: Beginning to Read) by Karen Wallace, Dorling Kindersley, 1999.

Honeybee's Busy Day by Richard Fowler, Harcourt, 1994. (ages 3 - 6)

The Honey Makers by Gail Gibbons, Morrow, William Co., 2000.

Horray for Beekeeping! by Niki Walker and Allison Larin, Crabtree Pub., 1997.

How Do Bees Make Honey? by Anna Claybourne, EDC Publications, 1995.

If You Should Hear a Honey Guide by April Pulley Sayre, Houghton Mifflin Co., 2000.

The Magic School Bus Inside a Beehive, created by Joanna Cole, Scholastic, 1996.

A Taste of Honey by Nancy Elizabeth Wallace, Winslow Press, 2001.

And Just for Fun

Winnie the Pooh and the Honey Tree, Walt Disney Video, 1965. VHS, UPC: 786936126815

National Courtesy Month

Don't pass up an opportunity to teach and reinforce good manners and social skills! Start with this bulletin board idea. You'll find patterns on pages 79-80. Then use the reproducibles on pages 81-88 for more learning opportunities.

Print the callouts on any brightly colored paper. Challenge your students to think of more "courtesy" words and add them to the bulletin board.

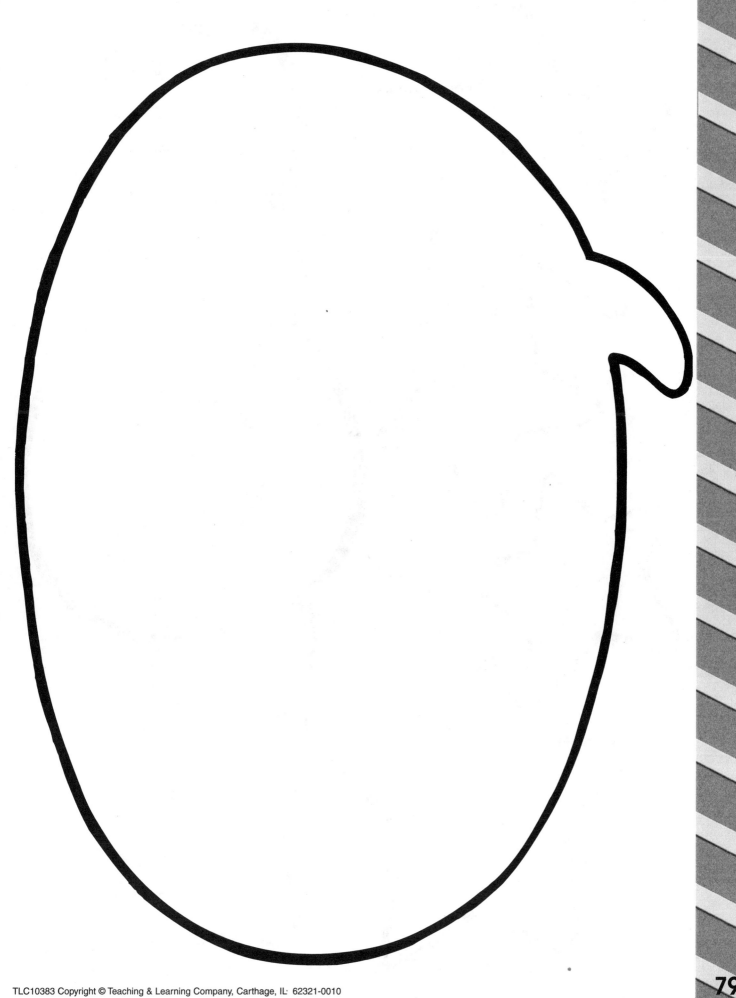

Name _____

Writing simple sentences

Juan and Hannah

Look at each picture. Read the question. Write an answer to the question on the line.

What will Juan say?

_____

Will Hannah help Jasmine?

_____

Writing simple sentences
Lily and Sam

Look at each picture. Read the question. Write an answer to the question on the line.

Will Lily pick up her toys?

_____

What will Sam do?

_____

The Right Words

Give each student a sheet of paper. Ask him to number it from 1 to 10 and write his name in the top left corner.

Now copy these four phrases and letters on the board:

A. "Excuse me, please."   B. "Thank you."   C. "I'm sorry."   D. "You're welcome."

Explain to the class that you are going to read them different situations, and they are to listen closely and decide which letter shows the right thing to say in that situation. Here's an example to read to the class:

You've just sneezed in a room full of people. What should you say?
Yes . . . the best answer is A. "Excuse me, please." For this item you would write A on your paper.

1. Ed needed to crawl over two friends at the theater in order to get to the aisle. (A)

2. Sachico's friend, Joe, just brought her three roses from his garden. She should say, (B). Then Joe should say, (D).

3. Matt forgot to do a chore his mother had asked him to do. (C)

4. Your teacher is talking with another teacher, but you need to ask a question about your worksheet. (A)

5. At the lunch table, Arnold accidentally let out a big burp. (A)

6. Luis's friend just paid for his meal. (B)

7. Your grandmother gave you a gift. (B)

8. Pedro just told Sal that his goldfish died. Sal should say, (C).

9. Your mother thanks you for setting the table. You should say, (D).

10. For the last item, choose one of the four phrases on the board. Turn your paper over and draw a picture of a situation in which someone should say the words you chose. Write those words under your picture.

Consider role playing with students using situations similar to the ones above in which students could practice doing and saying polite things.

Short on Manners

The word *manners* has a short *a* sound in the first syllable.
Here are more words with short vowel sounds:

cat

bed

pig

fox

cup

Look at each picture below. Say its name, and listen for the short vowel sound.
Circle the vowel that you hear.

a e i o u   a e i o u   a e i o u

a e i o u   a e i o u   a e i o u

a e i o u   a e i o u   a e i o u

a e i o u   a e i o u   a e i o u

Name _____

Nouns

Waiter, Waiter!

Waiters and waitresses are trained to be very helpful and polite to their customers.
Read these instructions that a restaurant owner might give to her new staff
members to help them become excellent waiters and waitresses.
Circle all the nouns you find. Remember that nouns are naming words.

1. Be sure the customer is seated comfortably in the chair.

2. Tell the customers where they may hang their coats.

3. Give every person a menu.

4. Ask parents if they want a highchair or coloring page and crayons for their children.

5. Find out what drink each guest would like.

6. Bring the coffee, tea, soda and water right away.

7. Serve milk with the meal.

8. Remember to give out cream and sugar for people who drink coffee or tea.

9. Ask what each person would like to order.

10. Write down the meals clearly and give the order to the cook.

11. Be sure to tell the guests, "Thank you," before they leave the table.

12. Write one more instruction you would give to a new waiter or waitress.

Addition
Order, Please!

Some very polite waiters and waitresses have been taking breakfast orders from their customers. The very busy cook must now figure out how many eggs and other items to cook. Read the orders carefully and then answer the questions.

Waitress: Sally

Table 1	Table 2	Table 3
2 scrambled eggs 2 sausages 2 pieces of toast 2 orange juice	3 scrambled eggs 2 pieces of toast 1 oatmeal 1 doughnut 3 orange juice	6 scrambled eggs 2 oatmeal 2 sausages 5 pieces of toast 3 doughnuts 4 orange juice

Waiter: Henry

Table 4	Table 5	Table 6
4 scrambled eggs 6 sausages 3 pieces of toast 3 orange juice	3 scrambled eggs 4 oatmeal 4 pieces of toast 5 orange juice	2 scrambled eggs 2 sausages 2 pieces of toast 1 orange juice

1. How many eggs does the chef need to cook for Sally's customers? _____

2. How many eggs does he need to cook for Henry's customers? _____

3. How many eggs does he need to cook in all? _____

4. How many bowls of oatmeal are needed for all six tables? _____

5. How many sausages are needed in all? _____

6. How many glasses of orange juice does Henry need? _____

7. How many glasses of orange juice does Sally need? _____

8. How many doughnuts does Henry need? _____

Name _____

O.J. Orders

Look on the previous page at the orders that Sally and Henry took.
Each table ordered orange juice. Complete this bar graph to show
how much orange juices were ordered at each table.

Table 1						
Table 2						
Table 3						
Table 4						
Table 5						
Table 6						
Number of glasses of orange juice	1	2	3	4	5	6

On the back of this page, draw a picture of your favorite breakfast foods.

Logic, using a chart
The Lunch Bunch

Four friends go out to lunch together every week. They are careful to use their very best manners with each other. Look at the pictures and read the clues to figure out which person is having which meal. Finish the chart. Write the person's name under the correct meal.

1. Everyone has fruit.
2. Maria has a salad.
3. Dan has a pickle.
4. Tim has juice.

	milk	juice	sandwich	salad	fruit	pickle
Dan					X	
Maria				X	X	
Rosa					X	
Tim					X	

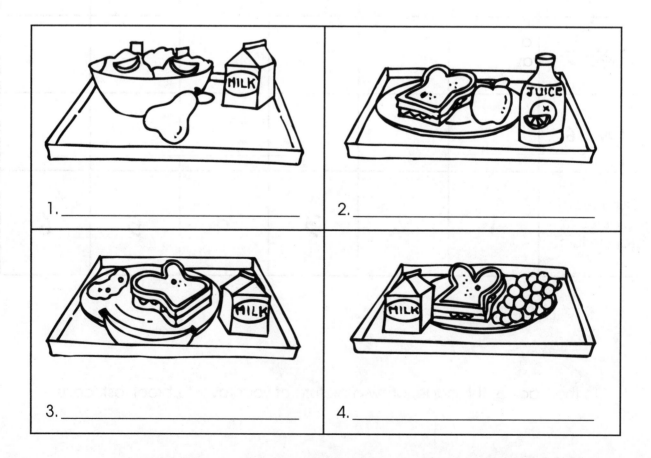

1. _____

2. _____

3. _____

4. _____

Happy Labor Day!

Labor Day is a holiday celebrated on the first Monday in September in the United States, Canada and other countries. The first Labor Day celebration was in 1882 when the Knights of Labor held a huge parade in New York City. In 1892, the U.S. Congress made it a legal holiday. This is a day to honor workers of all kinds, and celebrations often include speeches, political rallies, cookouts and parades. Although you probably won't be holding class on Labor Day, your class can still participate in many activities related to this special day on other days in September. Here are some ideas:

- Use the bulletin board on the page that follows to talk about different hats and uniforms worn by some workers.

- Let students share information about the jobs held by family members. The parent letter on page 93 will help you gather interesting information. (Please note that you are free to change the letter in any way you choose.)

- After reading the parent responses, you may wish to try to schedule one of them to come in and speak to the class about his or her work. Or you may want to ask a parent to send some special tools or uniforms to school for "show and tell."

- Hold a brainstorming session with your students. Ask them to list every job they can. Will your class be able to fill the entire chalkboard? You may wish to make a copy of this list on paper as a reference, such as for future report topics, etc.

- Hold your own pre- or post-Labor Day parade. Ask each student to represent an occupation of his choice. Each student should draw a picture of something that relates to his job and carry it while the class marches around inside the classroom or outside the school building.

- Find out if your students can visit a nearby workplace such as a fire station, retail store or hospital. Arrange ahead of time for a guided tour and parent volunteers to help chaperone. Help your students to learn about the workers' jobs, their special skills and training, and the tools they use.

- Check out one or more of these books to read to your class:

Career Day by Anne F. Rockwell, HarperCollins, 2000.

Jobs People Do by Christopher Maynard, Dorling Kindersley, 2001.

Labor Day by Carmen Bredeson, et al., Children's Press, 2001.

Labor Day by Mir Tamim Ansary, Heinnemann Library, 1998.

Our Neighborhood series from Children's Press.

Labor Day

Use patterns on pages 91-92 also on the CD. Give each child a hat to color and put on the board or they can make their own. If possible, find real hats to attach to the bulletin board or to place on a table nearby.

92

Date: _____

Dear Parents/Caregivers,

During the month of September we are learning about some of the different jobs held by people in our community. We know that Labor Day is one special day when all workers are honored, but we also want to honor and learn about workers among our families and friends during this month.

Please help us to learn more about one or more jobs by answering these questions. Then return the answers (on this paper or another piece) to school by _____.

1. What is the title of your job? What are your duties?

_____

_____

2. List any special tools you use.

_____

_____

3. List any special training you needed before starting this job.

_____

_____

4. What do you like best about your job?

_____

_____

Thank you for your cooperation. We look forward to learning more about your work!

Sincerely,

_____

Vocabulary, initial consonants
Worker Matchup

Draw a line from each beginning letter to a word.
Make the matches to spell the names of 10 different kinds of workers.

b   ___urse

t   ___armer

c   ___eacher

p   ___entist

n   ___ayor

d   ___anker

f   ___oach

l   ___ibrarian

d   ___river

m   ___olice officer

Name _____

Handwriting, creative thinking
When I Grow Up

Finish writing each sentence by supplying words of your own.
Use your best handwriting, and remember to use ending punctuation.

1. When I grow up, I might want to be a _____ or

   a _____ because _____

   _____

2. If I wanted to get one of these jobs, I would first need to _____

3. The best part about my "dream" job would be _____

   _____

4. I am quite sure I would never want to be a _____

   or a _____ because_____

   _____

5. Someone in my family works as _____

6. If I were a builder, I'd like to build _____

7. If I were a cook, I'd like to make _____

8. If I were a reporter I'd like to travel to _____

   and learn about _____

9. When I earn enough money, I'd like to buy _____

Name _____

Tool Time

Write the name of the worker under each picture who might use each tool.

fire fighter	hairdresser	waiter	musician
painter	gardener	carpenter	referee
cashier	doctor	cook	mail carrier

Counting by 10s

The Toes Know!

People have 10 toes each. Two people, then would have 20 toes, right?
Look at the rows of community workers. Read the number in each row.
Circle the number of people you would need to have that many toes.

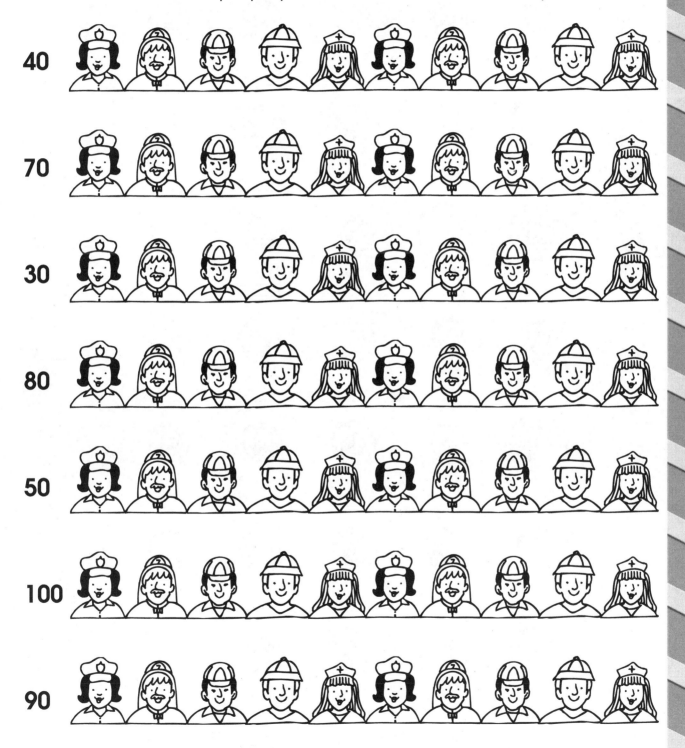

40

70

30

80

50

100

90

Name _____

Adding coin values

Time for Change

On Labor Day seven friends decided to go to work for themselves doing odd jobs for their neighbors. Each friend earned a few coins. Find the value of each set of coins.

Nick   = ____ ¢

____¢ ____¢ ____¢ ____¢ ____¢

Julia   = ____ ¢

____¢ ____¢ ____¢ ____¢

Josh   = ____ ¢

____¢ ____¢ ____¢ ____¢

Christie   = ____ ¢

____¢ ____¢ ____¢ ____¢ ____¢

Luke   = ____ ¢

____¢ ____¢ ____¢ ____¢ ____¢

Jacinda   = ____ ¢

____¢ ____¢ ____¢ ____¢ ____¢

Lisa   = ____ ¢

____¢ ____¢ ____¢ ____¢

Which friend made the most money? Circle the name.
Which friend made the least money? Draw a line under the name.

98

TLC10383 Copyright © Teaching & Learning Company, Carthage, IL 62321-0010

Grandparents' Day

Grandparents greatly enrich many children's lives. They often provide stability and encouragement in ways that other adults cannot. Take some time during September to remind students of these valuable relatives, and encourage them to show their appreciation to their grandparents.

The card on pages 100-101 is a great way to do this. Follow these instructions:

- Photocopy the two pages front to back so that page 100 is the outside of the card and page 101 is the inside of the card.

- Pass out the cards to students.

- Instruct students to color the letters on the front of the card.

- On the top inside, ask students to finish the sentence and illustrate it.

- On the bottom inside, help students think of words or phrases that begin with each letter to describe their grandparents. Here are some ideas: G–grand, generous, glorious, going all the time. R–readers, really wonderful, ready for fun, relaxing. E–exciting, extra-special, easy to love. A–awesome, above average, always there. T–terrific, tremendous, totally cool.

- On the back, have students sign their names and include the date.

- Be prepared with extra copies in case students want to make more cards at home for additional grandparents.

Consider holding a Grandparents' Open House. You will find a sample letter of invitation on page 102. Prepare students ahead of time on how to introduce their guests to the rest of the class. After the grandparents have arrived and been introduced, ask them to observe many of the things you do in a normal school day. Special activities are not necessary, so keep it simple! The "surprises" mentioned in the letter can be the handmade cards, a simple snack such as juice and pretzels and the singing of this fun new song: Our Grandparents Are Great! (Sung to the tune of "The Farmer in the Dell.")

> Our Grandparents are great!
> Our Grandparents are great!
> One, two, we know it's true
> Our Grandparents are great!

You'll also find the reproducibles on pages 103-107 to be full of ways to remind students of the wonderful grandparents in their lives.

Children whose grandparents are unavailable may wish to invite a parent or adult friend. These participants can be identified as "Grand Parent" or "Grand Friend" and hopefully, everyone will have a Grand Time!

Grandparents' Day

Date

Card written by

One of my favorite things to do with you is

Grandparents are

G _____

R _____

E _____

A _____

T _____

and that includes you!

Date: _____

Dear Grandparents:

You are very special! During September the students in our class are working on activities that remind us of how much we appreciate you.

We would like to invite you to visit our class on _____
date

at _____ .
time

This is a Grandparents' Open House. It is an invitation for you to see our classroom, meet our friends and watch us work. There may also be a surprise or two as well.

Please let me know by _____ if you can come to our special open house. I really hope you can!

Love,

_____

Name _____

Grandparents Are Great!

Grandparents and *great* both start with the same two letters.
Can you hear the *grrr* in other words, too, like *growl*? Read the words on the left.
Draw a line to match each word to the correct picture.

grass

grapes

groundhog

grill

grin

groceries

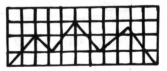

graph

grip

things that are green

Name _____

Long vowel words
What I Like

What do you like to do with your grandparents?
Here are answers from some children. Look at each picture and read the sentence.
Circle every word that has a long vowel sound.

> Remember that when a word has two vowels, the first one usually takes its long sound.
> The second vowel is silent, as in *gain, wheel, tie, boat, late* and *bike*.

1. We like to rake leaves.

2. My grandma and I like to bake pies.

3. My pap and I like to ice skate.

4. My gram and I like to try on clothes.

5. My grandpa and I play cards.

Name _____

Grandpa and I

A sentence tells a complete idea. Here is an example: *Grandpa is a great cook.*
The sentence is about Grandpa. It tells a complete idea about him.

This is not a sentence: *Grandpa*   It does not tell a complete idea.

Circle each sentence. Draw a picture for one of the sentences on the back.

1. Grandpa cooks eggs.

2. Scrambled eggs.

3. He makes ham and toast, too.

4. Buttery toast with jam.

5. Grandpa likes breakfast.

6. Grandpa cleans up the kitchen.

7. I like to help him.

8. Dirty pots and pans.

9. Going fishing this weekend.

10. We hope to catch two large fish.

11. Then Grandpa can cook fish, too.

12. Trout and bluegill.

Recognizing and counting basic shapes
Grandma's House

Don't you love to visit Grandma? Look at all the shapes hidden in this Grandma's house!
There are circles ●, squares ■, rectangles ▮ and triangles ▲.
Count the number of each shape. Write the numbers at the bottom.

How many circles? _____   How many rectangles? _____

How many squares? _____   How many triangles? _____

Addition and subtraction
Number Families

People live in families, and numbers do, too! Or at least they work together in groups.
For example, look at the way you can use the numbers 3, 4 and 7:

$$3 + 4 = 7 \qquad 7 - 4 = 3$$
$$4 + 3 = 7 \qquad 7 - 3 = 4$$

Show how these number families work.

6, 4, 10	**7, 5, 12**	**5, 6, 11**
$6 + 4 =$ _____	$5 +$ _____ $= 12$	____ $+$ ____ $=$ ____
$4 + 6 =$ _____	$7 +$ _____ $= 12$	____ $+$ ____ $=$ ____
$10 - 6 =$ _____	$12 - 5 =$ _____	$11 - 6 =$ _____
$10 - 4 =$ _____	_____ $- 7 = 5$	____ $- 5 =$ ____
9, 7, 16	**5, 8, 13**	**3, 9, 12**
____ $+$ ____ $=$ ____	____ $+$ ____ $=$ ____	____ $+$ ____ $=$ ____
____ $+$ ____ $=$ ____	____ $+$ ____ $=$ ____	____ $+$ ____ $=$ ____
____ $-$ ____ $=$ ____	____ $-$ ____ $=$ ____	____ $-$ ____ $=$ ____
____ $-$ ____ $=$ ____	____ $-$ ____ $=$ ____	____ $-$ ____ $=$ ____
8, 7, 15	**3, 6, 9**	**6, 8, 14**
____ $+$ ____ $=$ ____	____ $+$ ____ $=$ ____	____ $+$ ____ $=$ ____
____ $+$ ____ $=$ ____	____ $+$ ____ $=$ ____	____ $+$ ____ $=$ ____
____ $-$ ____ $=$ ____	____ $-$ ____ $=$ ____	____ $-$ ____ $=$ ____
____ $-$ ____ $=$ ____	____ $-$ ____ $=$ ____	____ $-$ ____ $=$ ____

Note to teachers and parents: Mexico fought for and gained its independence in the early 1800s. On the night before September 16, 1810, the priest Miguel Hidalgo y Costilla rang his church's bells and encouraged the local Indians to reclaim their land from the Spaniards. Today, September 16 is celebrated as Mexican Independence Day.

Mexican Music

Many, many years ago church bells in Mexico rang out, calling people to take their own land back from Spain. Look closely at these bells. Find the two that are exactly the same. Circle these two bells. Color all the rest.

Name _____

Mexican Sets

Look at these number words. They are written in both Spanish and English.
Count the number of objects in each set. Write the correct word in both languages
in the blank. Practice saying the new words with your teacher and classmates.

uno = one	tres = three	cinco = five	siete = seven	nueve = nine
dos = two	cuatro = four	seis = six	ocho = eight	diez = ten

_____   _____   _____

_____   _____   _____

   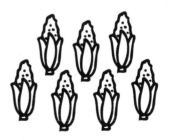

_____   _____   _____

Name _____

Color words

Spanish Color Words

Mexican Independence Day is a great time to learn color words, both in English and Spanish. Look at the word written in Spanish on each crayon. Follow the letters along each line. Write the letters that you find in the blank at the bottom of the page. Read the color word in English. Color each crayon the correct color.

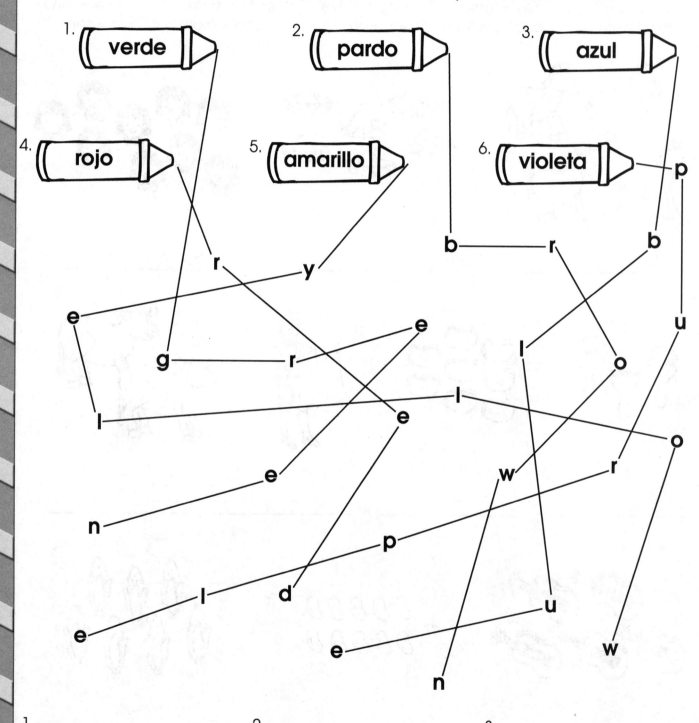

1. verde
2. pardo
3. azul
4. rojo
5. amarillo
6. violeta

1. _____   2. _____   3. _____

4. _____   5. _____   6. _____

Name _____

At the End

Here are some things you might see at a Mexican celebration.
Circle the consonant sound that you hear at the end of each word.

b   l   s   t   f   g   r   n   b   g   n   t

d   r   t   w   d   m   n   s   g   k   m   t

b   j   m   r   f   l   p   t   h   m   p   r

Name _____

Mexican Map

Follow these directions to label your own map of Mexico.

1. Write *NORTH* at the top of this map.
2. Write *SOUTH* at the bottom.
3. Write *WEST* at the left side of this map.
4. Write *EAST* at the right side.
5. Write *U.S.A.* in the land area north of Mexico.
6. Write *Pacific Ocean* in the water to the west of Mexico.
7. Write *Gulf of Mexico* in the water to the east of Mexico.
8. Write *Mexico City* by the star to show the name of Mexico's capital city.

Mexico

Elephant Appreciation Day

Did you know that elephants have their very own day of appreciation? It's on September 22. Learn along with your students about these amazing animals, the largest ones that live on land. This would be a great month to visit a zoo and observe elephants up close.

Use the reproducibles on the pages that follow to teach important skills and learn more about elephants. The factual article on page 115 can be read aloud with students if the difficulty level is too high for younger children.

Here are just a few of the many children's books about elephants, both silly and serious, to supplement your classroom library during September. Most are for ages 4-8.

Non-Fiction

African Elephants by Roland Smith. The Lerner Publishing Group, 1995.

Elephants for Kids by Anthony D. Fredericks. Creative Publishing International, 1999.

Elephants: Life in the Wild by Monica Kulling. Golden Books Publishing, 2000.

The Elephant, Peaceful Giant by Christine and Michel Denis-Huot. Charlesbridge Publishing, 1992.

Through Tsavo: A Story of an East African Savanna by Schuyler M. Bull. Soundprints, 1998.

Fiction

Elmer by David McKee. Morrow, William, and Co., 1991.

I'm Too Big (Soy Demasiado Grande) by Lone Morton, et al. Barron's Educational Series, Inc., 1994.

Just a Little Bit by Ann Tompert. Houghton Mifflin, 1996.

"Stand Back" Said the Elephant, "I'm Going to Sneeze!" by Patricia Thomas, HarperCollins, 1991.

The Story of Babar: The Little Elephant by Jean deBrunhoff. Random House, 1976.

When the Elephant Walks by Keiko Kasza. The Putnam Publishing Group, 1997.

Joke Book

Elephantastic! A trunkful of Unforgettable Jokes by Diana Newton-Hurt. Larousse Kingfisher Chambers, Inc., 1995.

Shape Book Pattern

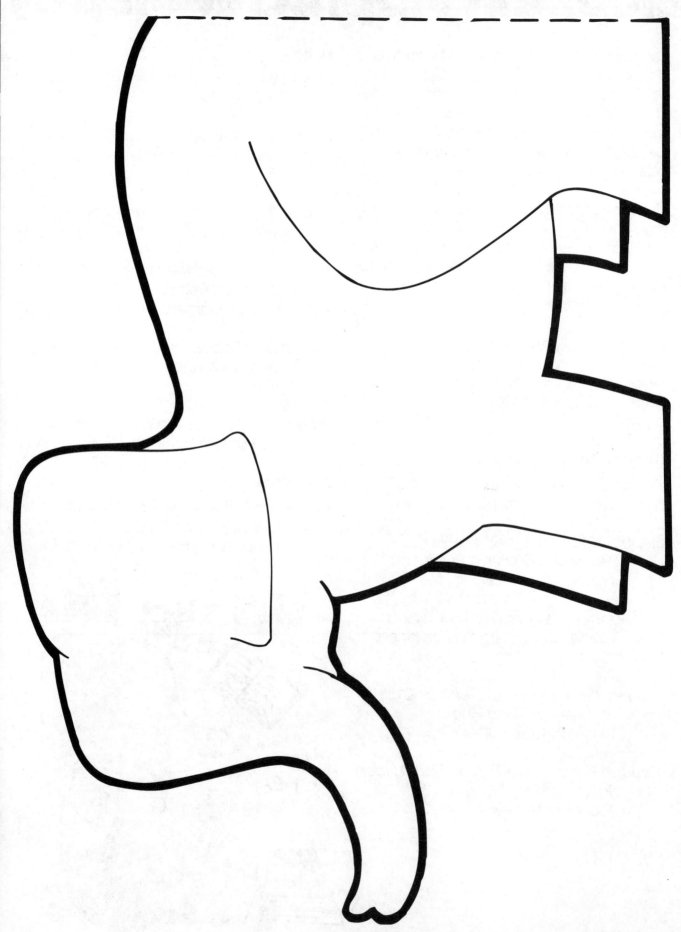

Name _____

Reading comprehension
Elephant Info

Read this article about elephants. Then answer the questions at the bottom of the page.

> Elephants are fun to see at a circus or in a zoo. The elephant is the largest animal that lives on land. It is very smart and very strong, and its body is truly amazing. Perhaps the most interesting part on an elephant's body is its trunk.
>
> An elephant uses its trunk to feed itself and to drink water. The trunk is long enough to reach up into trees and grab fruit, shoots and leaves. The trunk then places the food into the elephant's mouth. To drink water, the elephant sucks up water in its trunk and then squirts the water into its mouth. It does not drink through its trunk.
>
> The trunk also helps an elephant to take a bath. It sucks up water in its trunk and then sprays it all over the rest of its body. Would you like to take a bath that way?
>
> The elephant even uses its trunk to greet other elephants in its herd. Of course, since the trunk has two nostrils on the end, the elephant uses its trunk for smelling, too.

1. A good title for the article would be:

    a. Circus Elephants

    b. Elephants Are Strong

    c. Elephants' Amazing Trunks

2. Circle every use for an elephant's trunk that is mentioned in the article:

    a. reaches food from trees   d. puts food into its mouth

    b. drinks water   e. squirts water on its body

    c. greets other elephants   f. chews food

3. How do we know an elephant uses its trunk to smell?_____

_____

4. What are the two things the elephant does in order to get a drink of water.

    _____   _____

5. What kind of food does an elephant get from a tree? _____

6. Underline one sentence in the article that tells something new you learned.

Name _____

Ask and Tell

A sentence tells a complete idea. Here are two special kinds of sentences:

A statement is a sentence that tells something. It ends in a period (.).
A question is a sentence that asks something. It ends in a question mark (?).

Write S in front of each statement. Put a period at the end.
Write Q in front of each question. Put a question mark at the end.

____ Have you ever seen an elephant

____ There are two types of elephants

____ The Asian elephant is also called the Indian elephant

____ The other kind of elephant is the African elephant

____ Which kind of elephant is larger

____ African elephants are slightly larger than Asian elephants

____ Which elephant has bigger ears

____ The African elephant's ears are much larger

____ Elephants are endangered animals

____ Some are killed for their ivory tusks

____ Will the number of living elephants increase

____ Some elephants live on reserves where they are protected

Name _____

Writing statements and questions
Circus Scene

Look at this circus scene. Think about what is happening. Then write two statements and two questions to go with the picture. Use words from the box to help you.

elephant	acrobat	ringmaster	trainer
clown	seal	trapeze	peanuts

Statement: _____

Question: _____

Statement: _____

Question: _____

Reading scales, completing a bar graph
Weigh to Go!

Each elephant is sitting on a very sturdy set of scales. Read each one and color in the bar graph at the bottom of the page to show how much each one weighs. Put a number in each box to show the order of their weights. Put a 1 in the box by the elephant who weighs the most. Put a 6 in the box to show who weighs the least.

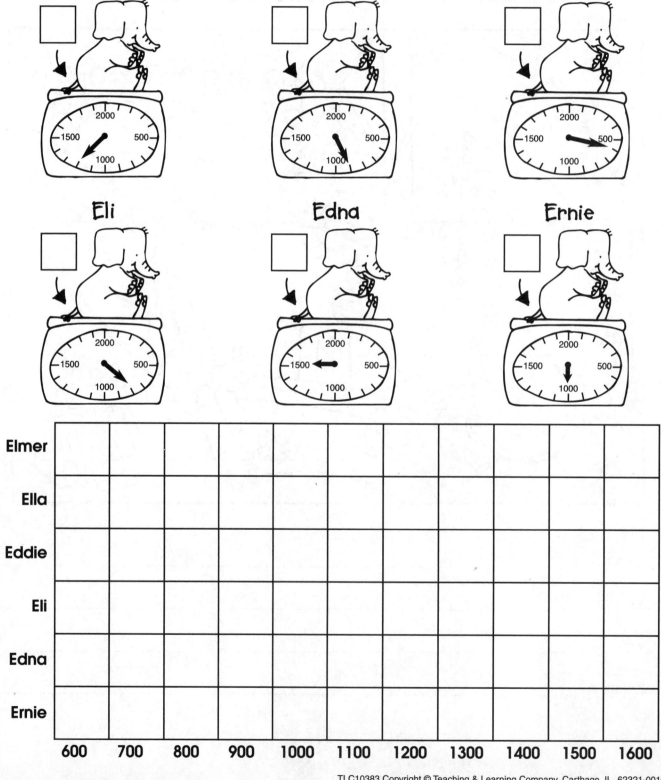

TLC10383 Copyright © Teaching & Learning Company, Carthage, IL 62321-0010

Name _____

Four Score

Maybe you've eaten elephant ears at a fair or amusement park. Here is one that has been divided into fourths. If four friends were sharing this, each one would receive one part. Each person would have the same amount of the elephant ear. Color $1/4$ of the elephant ear.

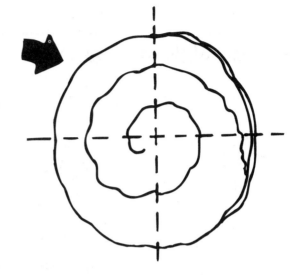

Here is an elephant-sized sandwich! Color $2/4$ of the sandwich. Can you see it is the same as $1/2$?

Here is a shady spot where four elephant friends can sit. If they don't want to touch each other, each will need his own space. Can you divide this space into four equal parts? Color $3/4$ of the parts that you make.

Here is a huge shoot from a plant that elephants like to eat. Can you divide it into four even parts so that four elephant friends can all eat the same amount? Color $1/4$ of the parts.

Animal classification

Bone Zone

Look at the animals in the boxes. Answer the questions below.

Animals Without a Backbone	Animals with a Backbone
earthworm	elephant
starfish	turtle
snail	fish
clam	bird
spider	person
insect	snake

1. Circle the animal without a backbone that lives in the ground.

2. Draw a line under all animals that live in the water all of the time.

3. Circle the largest animal that lives on the land.

4. Put an X next to all the animals that have legs.

5. Color all the animals that you have seen.

Drawing, symmetry
Be an Elephant Artist

Look at this elephant. Half of him is missing!
Try to draw the rest of this elephant so that both sides look the same.

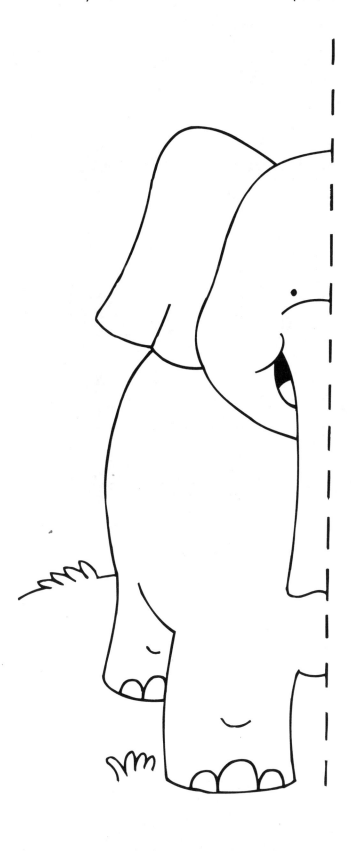

All-Purpose September

Use a bright fall color for the background, such as gold or orange, and a contrasting color for lettering. See the patterns on pages 123-124. Consider using colored leaves, bees or apples for a border.

Honey Month

Labor Day

Grandparents' Day

Mexican Independence Day

Elephant Appreciation Day

Courtesy Month

September News

Bookmarks

Use these bookmarks during the special days in September.

Let's Make a "Bee" Line for a Book!

Read a Book with a Grandparent

Visit Mexico with a Book!

I'm Tracking Elephants in Books!

October

Get ready for an outstanding October with six special themes: National Cookie Month, National Stamp Collecting Month, Fire Prevention Week, Columbus Day, Dictionary Day and, of course, Halloween. For some of these themes you will find bulletin boards and resource lists. For others you might see a student game idea, or a story to read. For all of the units you will have appealing reproducibles that cover important primary-grade skills. An answer key is included at the end of the book.

You can copy the reproducible pages directly from the book. The bulletin board patterns, stationery and other items are included on the CD and numbered for easy reference.

First your students will savor the fun and learning of National Cookie Month. This section includes a bulletin board idea, a crossword puzzle, a counting page and other math and language activities. This section ends with recipes and ideas for a cookie party.

For National Stamp Collecting Month, you may want to send your students a post-card through the "real" mail. A reproducible is included. You will find pages featuring phonics, sentence skills, rhyming words, number patterns and addition. A special activity at the end of this section teaches kids about flow charts.

Fire Prevention Week begins with a bright bulletin board, safety rules and facts about Dalmatians. Students will solve a maze, finish drawing a fire truck and complete word problems.

Columbus Day brings a word search, historical facts, a listening lesson and more.

A brief section for Dictionary Day supplies ideas for student dictionary games and reproducibles featuring alphabetical order.

Halloween is the last special section. Begin with a bulletin board, custom-made by your students. You will also find a board game and skill pages covering thirds, coins, reading comprehension and more.

The final pages contain bookmarks to be used throughout the month as well as an all-purpose stationery page. Don't forget all the great clip art on the CD. It promises to make for a truly outstanding October in your classroom!

National Cookie Month

Use the irresistible topic of cookies to teach some important skills during the month of October. Included in this unit are skill pages for noting details and practicing phonics, vocabulary, counting, addition and more. And what would a cookie unit be without some recipes? Check out our no-bake recipes on page 137. Remember that students can learn valuable skills as they read directions and measure ingredients.

In addition to the skill pages that follow, here are some more cookie-learning math ideas:

• With students of any age, you can practice English measurements used in cooking. Show students measuring cups and spoons. Take some time to "play" at the sink measuring water. Can they find out how many cups of water it takes to fill a quart measuring pitcher? They can also measure to find out how many tablespoons are in a cup and so on.

• Take a survey among your students. Ask if students prefer chocolate chip, peanut butter or sugar cookies (or other options of your choice). Record the survey results in a chart, and show the class how to present the same information in a graph. Picture graphs, circle graphs or bar graphs would work well. You may want to make one large graph altogether to post on a classroom wall. As a follow-up, ask students to individually take their own surveys. Tell them to ask 10 people in their home or school to tell their favorite kind of cookie. Instruct students to return surveys to class where you can help them complete their own personal graph.

• Learn about unit pricing. Bring in three different packages of purchased cookies, along with the price of each. Do three division problems on the chalkboard to compare which type costs most and least per cookie. Once you've determined the unit price for/with students, ask them to multiply to find the price of 3, 5, 10 or 20 cookies.

Bulletin Board Idea

Select a bright green, blue or orange color for background. Post the words *We Love Cookies!* in the center of the board. Ask students to cut out large cookie shapes from white, beige or brown paper and decorate them to look like their favorite cookies. They should include on the front the name of this type of cookie, along with their name. Add these cut-outs to the bulletin board. For a cute border, use colors that contrast with your background. Ask students to trace various cookie cutters and cut out the shapes. Help students add the border pieces to the bulletin board, arranging them in a pattern, if possible.

Name _____

Cut-Out Cookies

Amber made a lot of cut-out cookies.
Can you find nine cookies that are just like this one?

Circle the nine cookies that match.
Color the other cookies.

Phonics—hard and soft c
C Is for Cookie

The sound that *c* makes at the beginning of *cookie* is called the hard sound.
The sound that *c* makes at the beginning of *cereal* is called the soft sound.
Usually, if *c* is followed by *e, i* or *y*, it has the soft sound. Look at the picture and
say the word in each box. Underline the word if it has the hard sound as in *cookie*.
Circle the word if it has the soft sound as in *cereal*.

cow	cymbals	cake
camera	computer	cent
circle	corn	cup

Now color all the pictures.

TLC10383 Copyright © Teaching & Learning Company, Carthage, IL 62321-0010

Name _____

Long e sound
Cookie, Please!

Both the words *cookie* and *please* have the long e sound, but the sound is spelled in two different ways. There are other ways to spell the long e sound, too. Look at these words:

key   sheep   piece   puppy   me

All have the long e sound, and all are spelled differently.

Read each clue below. Write the answers in the puzzle.
Each answer is a word that has a long e sound. Use the word list if you need help.
It contains extra words, so remember to use only the long e words.

Word List

leg	feet
green	brown
peep	keep
cash	money
chirp	hold
talk	speak
eagle	flee
stop	yield
geese	team
people	men

Across
2. the color of grass
3. to talk
6. people who play a sport together
9. sound baby birds make
10. to leave quickly
11. word on a traffic sign

Down
1. what you walk with
2. more than one goose
4. persons
5. to save something
7. large bird
8. what you spend

Cookie Party!

Look at the picture of the class having a cookie party. Doesn't it look like fun?
Read each sentence. If it is a statement, rewrite it as a question.
If it is a question, rewrite it as a statement. One example is done for you.

1. This is a cookie party.

    Is this a cookie party?

2. Is the punch yummy?

   _____

3. There are many people at the party.

   _____

4. The best cookie is the snickerdoodle.

   _____

5. Does Ramon like lemon the best?

   _____

6. Will you come to my party next week?

   _____

7. This party is fun.

   _____

Name _____

Vocabulary
Tasty Treats

What is your favorite kind of cookie? How would you describe it? You could say the cookie is good. Or you could say it is delicious, chewy and fresh-baked. These are big words, but they tell more than just the word *good*. Think about each food that's listed below. Write three more words of your choice that tell more about it.

1. Chocolate chip cookie: sweet, _____, _____, _____

2. Vanilla ice cream: cold, _____, _____, _____

3. Fresh-picked apple: crisp, _____, _____, _____

4. Sweet corn: messy, _____, _____, _____

5. Tossed salad: green, _____, _____, _____

6. Hot dog: chewy, _____, _____, _____

7. Strawberries: juicy, _____, _____, _____

8. Milk shake: thick, _____, _____, _____

9. Taco: crunchy, _____, _____, _____

Counting by fives
Cookie Count

Each cookie has five chocolate chips. Count by fives to learn how many chocolate chips are on this page. Write the missing numbers in the blanks.

 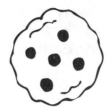 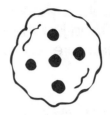 

5   _____   15   _____

25   30   _____   _____

45   _____   _____   60

_____   70   _____   80

 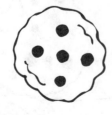  

85   _____   95   _____

Addition and subtraction
Cookie Trail

Bingo the Bear is on a cookie trail! He is walking through a magical forest where there are cookies all around. But he is also very hungry, so he is stopping to eat a lot along the way. Follow the path through the forest to learn how many cookies Bingo has. Add numerals to write the missing sums. Subtract numerals to write the differences.

Recipes and Party Ideas

National Cookie Month is a great time to get students involved in reading and following instructions. Several no-bake recipes are included on page 137, but you may prefer to have students do some actual baking. Before you start a classroom bake-off, consider these ideas:

- Ask for parent volunteers to help by coming into the classroom on your baking day. Some can take cookie sheets to the school kitchen if necessary to handle pans in and out of the oven. Others can stay in the classroom and help with the measuring and mixing.

- Ask students to bring in favorite family cookie recipes in advance. Send a note home suggesting families send in recipes that are easy to make, with ingredients that are easily obtainable and appealing to kids. Have students vote to select two or three they want to make together. Or, select two or three of your own personal favorite recipes and ask families to contribute ingredients.

- To save time, skip the measuring and mixing, and just do the baking and decorating if desired. Buy already pre-pared cookie dough and let your students roll, cut and decorate the dough.

- Consider adding non-sweet "cookies" to your party menu. Use cookie cutters to cut out fun shapes from sliced bread. Spread the bread with mar-garine, peanut butter or cheese.

- Hold a cookie exchange. Ask parents in advance to send in enough cookies to share one with each child. For example, in a class of 24 students, ask families to send in 24 cookies each. On the day of the party, spread all 24 kinds out on trays, waxed paper or paper towels. Give each student a resealable plastic bag or a foil-lined shoe box. After each child has washed his hands, instruct him to walk down the row of cookie trays and carefully take one cookie from each tray and put it in his box. Then each child can take home the same number of cookies that he brought, but now he will have 24 different kinds. Limit students to just one or two cookies to be eaten in class.

- Supplement the bread-spread "cookies" and sweet cookies with some raw vegetables, such as carrots, celery and cauliflower.

- Play the Cookie Cutter game. Say, "Have you ever noticed that when you cut out a lot of cookies with the same cookie cutter, they all have the same shape? People are not like cookie cutters, because none of us are exactly the same. Try your best, however, to look like cookie cutters. I am going to play some music. When the music stops, I want everyone to freeze. I will tap one of you on the shoulder. She will be our pretend cook-ie cutter. When you see the person I tap, you must all try to make yourself look like our cookie cutter. If her right arm is up in the air, you must put your right arm up in the air and so on."

Here are some easy, no-bake recipes. Always be sure to have potholders available, and remember to check all children's food allergies before serving any foods.

Crunchy Peanut Butter No-Bakes

Makes about 20-24 cookies.

1/2 cup corn syrup
1 cup sugar
2 cups peanut butter
2 cups chow mein noodles

Mix the corn syrup and sugar together in a pan. Heat on burner at a medium temperature until bubbly. Take the pan off the heat. Stir in peanut butter and noodles. Drop cookie batter from a spoon onto waxed paper. Cool for 15 minutes (or more) before eating.

Everybody's Favorite

1/4 (1/2 a stick) cup margarine
4 cups miniature marshmallows
5 cups crisp rice cereal

Melt the margarine over the stove in a three-quart saucepan. Add marshmallows and cook over low heat, stirring constantly. When the marshmallows are melted and syrupy, remove the pan from the heat. Add the cereal and stir until well coated. Press the warm mixture evenly into buttered 9" x13" pan. Cut into squares when cool. Note: You may also add raisins, chocolate chips or m&ms™ after the cereal.

Cornflake Cookies

1 cup brown sugar
1 cup peanut butter
1 cup corn syrup
2 cups salted peanuts
10 cups cornflakes

Moonballs

This one requires no cooking!
Makes 12-15 cookies, depending on size.

1 cup peanut butter
1/2 cup honey
1 cup instant dry milk powder
1/2 cup raisins
1 cup cereal, crushed

Mix the first four ingredients in a bowl. Form into balls and roll in crushed cereal. Enjoy!

Microwave One-Dish Brownies

1/2 cup margarine
6 tablespoons baking cocoa
1 cup sugar

Place margarine in an 8" square microwavable dish. Microwave on high for about one minute, or until it melts. Add cocoa and sugar and stir until smooth.

Add these ingredients in the order given and mix well:

1 egg
1 teaspoon vanilla
3/4 cup flour
1/2 teaspoon baking powder
1/4 teaspoon salt
1/2 cup chopped nuts (optional)

Microwave 5-6 minutes, rotating the dish a half turn after 2, 4 and 5 minutes. Cook until the brownies are no longer moist. Cool and serve. Cut into 16 small brownies.

Combine sugar, peanut butter and corn syrup in a large saucepan. Cook over medium heat and stir until mixture begins to bubble. Remove from heat. Stir in peanuts and cornflakes. Press warm mixture firmly into buttered 9" x 13" or 10" x 15" pan. Cool. Cut into desired number of pieces. *Note: These are very chewy. Small pieces are best!*

National Stamp Collecting Month

All kids love to get "real" mail! Start building your students' interest in the topic of National Stamp Collecting Month by mailing each one a postcard before the beginning of October. Read the rest of this page for more information on this special mailing as well as important student activities. Then complete the appealing skill pages from pages 140-146. Help students think logically and sequentially as you present the flow chart activities on page 147. Don't miss the list of resource books on stamp collecting and mail on page 148.

- Mail each child a postcard at his home address prior to the start of this unit. Use the reproducible on page 139. Photocopy this page onto stiff paper, then cut on the lines to match the size of a regular postcard. Sign your name on the back, and address the front of each card. Purchase postcard stamps at your local post office. (If possible, buy a variety of designs.)

- When students bring in their postcards, look at the postmarks together. These marks show the date and the place from which the card was mailed. Also see how the stamps are cancelled. This prevents them from being used again. Look at the other stamps students have brought in from other mail they have received at home. Are they all cancelled in the same way? Are all the stamps worth the same amount of money? In what different ways can the stamps be sorted?

- Ask students to practice addressing and stamping envelopes. Cut slips of paper the same size as business envelopes. Practice writing delivery and return addresses in the correct places, and in the correct format. Give students stickers to place in the upper right-hand corner on the "envelopes" that they correctly address.

Interesting Postal Facts

✉ The first postage stamps appeared in Britain in 1840. Postage cost one penny no matter how the letter had to travel.

✉ The Untied States started making its own stamps in 1847.

✉ Today, every country produces stamps in a range of prices. The weight of mail and the speed of delivery determine the price of the postage.

✉ Countries often honor its national events and famous citizens with their stamps.

✉ The postcard was invented in 1869 by Emmanual Hermann of Vienna.

✉ The first picture postcard was produced in 1894.

Dear

Surprise! This is a special postcard from your teacher. I wanted to let you and your family know that we will soon be learning about National Stamp Collecting Month. During October, we will learn about stamps and stamp collecting. We will also do skill pages related to stamps.

Please bring this postcard to school on or before October 1 for some special activities. You may also want to save other stamps from other mail to bring in to show the class. Here's to a great stamp-collecting month!

Sincerely,

Dear

Surprise! This is a special postcard from your teacher. I wanted to let you and your family know that we will soon be learning about National Stamp Collecting Month. During October, we will learn about stamps and stamp collecting. We will also do skill pages related to stamps.

Please bring this postcard to school on or before October 1 for some special activities. You may also want to save other stamps from other mail to bring in to show the class. Here's to a great stamp-collecting month!

Sincerely,

Dear _____,

Surprise! This is a special postcard from your teacher. I wanted to let you and your family know that we will soon be learning about National Stamp Collecting Month. During October, we will learn about stamps and stamp collecting. We will also do skill pages related to stamps.

Please bring this postcard to school on or before October 1 for some special activities. You may also want to save other stamps from other mail to bring in to show the class. Here's to a great stamp-collecting month!

Sincerely,

_____

Creative thinking
Stamp Designer

Interesting stamps have been created about many, many different themes.
Choose an item in each category listed below,
and then design a new stamp for each one. Color your new stamps.

Animal	Famous Person
Country	Job

Name _____

A Stamp Story

Read this story. Then answer the questions at the bottom.

Hi! My name is Betsy. I started collecting stamps two years ago, when I was six years old. I work on my stamp collection every Saturday. During the week, my mom saves all the stamps that are on the mail that comes to my house. On Saturdays, my brother helps me cut out the stamps and glue them into my special book.

Sometimes we go to a store that sells stamps for stamp collectors. My dad gives me one dollar to spend on stamps that I like. These are special stamps that have never been used on mail, so there are no marks on them and no envelopes stuck to the back of them. Sometimes I get stamps about cats or dogs. Sometimes I get stamps about the moon. My favorite stamps are the ones about flags. I have flags from 12 different countries in my stamp collection. Someday I hope to have even more!

1. A good title for this story would be:
   a. A Family Stamp Collection
   b. Stamps About Flags
   c. Betsy's Stamp Collection

2. How old is Betsy now? _____

3. Do you think Betsy likes to collect stamps? Why or why not?_____

_____

4. Who helps Betsy glue her stamps into her book? _____

5. What does Betsy's mom do to help her collect stamps?_____

_____

6. What kind of animal stamps does Betsy collect? _____

7. What kind of stamps do you think Betsy wants to get more of? _____

Name _____

Stamp Rhymes

Think of words that you know that rhyme with *stamp*. List some of them here:

_____

Now read the poem. Use the clues in each line to help you figure out the missing word.
Each missing word rhymes with *stamp*.

1. When something is not quite dry,

   We say that it's still _____ .

2. When Dad glues legs back onto a chair

   He holds them with a _____ .

3. In the summer we like to pack our tents

   To fish and hike and _____ .

4. A light in our living room

   Is usually called a _____ .

5. In a large parking garage we drive to the top

   On a winding parking _____ .

Draw a picture of one of your words on the back of this page.

If you still need help, here are some words you may use. There is one extra.

clamp   ramp   damp   camp   amp   lamp

Missing Letters

If the mail carrier has missing letters, that's a problem! If these words have missing letters, that's no problem, because you can find them. Say the name of each picture. Listen for all the letter sounds. Write the missing letter in each word.

__ ail

stam __

ca __

__ etter

do __

fl __ g

ca __

b __ x

v __ n

foo __

__ eg

shir __

Exclamations and commands
Surprise!

You may already know that all sentences begin with a capital letter. Many sentences end with a period. Some do not. Some sentences show surprise or strong feelings. These sentences should end with an exclamation mark (!).
Grandma gave me a whole set of new stamps for my stamp collection!

Some sentences give orders or commands. End most of these with a period.
Please put your stamps away.

If the order is urgent, you should use an exclamation at the end.
Watch out for that snake!

Copy each sentence on the line following it. Begin each one with a capital letter. Add a period or an exclamation mark at the end of each sentence.

1. please close the window _____

2. that wind is going to blow my stamps everywhere

_____

3. I must find an answer to this riddle tonight

_____

4. set the table, please_____

5. Dad just gave me five dollars for new stamps

_____

6. thank you, Dad _____

7. don't put your feet on the table

_____

8. get this cat out of my stamp collection

_____

9. please take me to the store

_____

Name _____

Stuck on Stamps

Each row of stamps shows a number pattern. Find out what the pattern is,
then write in the number that comes next on the last stamp.

    1. ☐

    2. ☐

     3. ☐

    4. ☐

    5. ☐

    6. ☐

    7. ☐

Name _____

Addition

Stampwork

Here is a nice collection of stamps. Pretend that you are going to mail letters and packages that cost different amounts. Which of these stamps will you need? Write the value of the stamps that you need to use in the blanks. The first one is done for you as an example. Use only one of each kind of stamp.

1. 60¢ _____ 57¢ + 3¢ _____

2. 32¢ _____

3. 25¢ _____

4. 56¢ _____

5. 37¢ _____

6. 13¢ _____

7. 79¢ _____

8. 67¢ _____

Now find three stamps for these sums:

9. 35¢ _____

10. 66¢ _____

Name _____

Go with the Flow

You know that you must follow several steps in the correct order to mail a letter.
This flow chart shows how to do that.

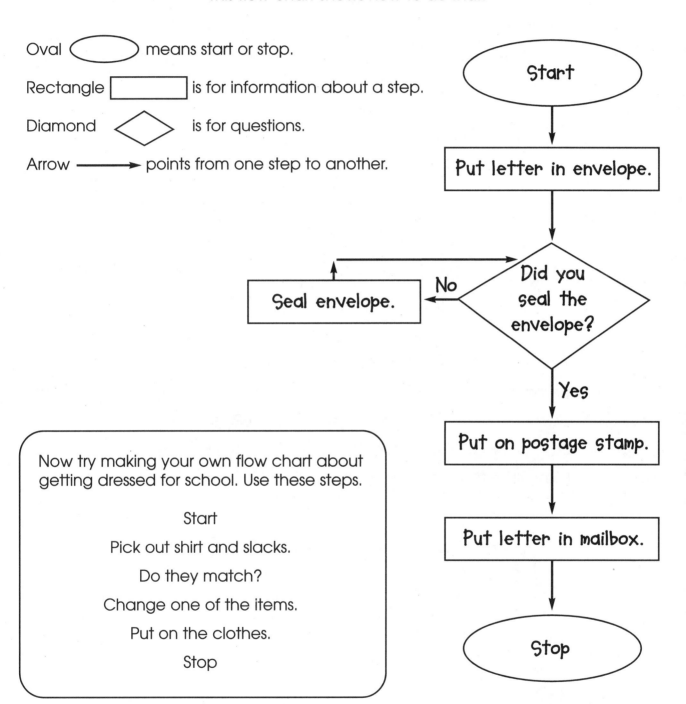

Oval ⬭ means start or stop.

Rectangle ▭ is for information about a step.

Diamond ◇ is for questions.

Arrow ⟶ points from one step to another.

Start

Put letter in envelope.

Did you seal the envelope?

No → Seal envelope.

Yes

Put on postage stamp.

Put letter in mailbox.

Stop

Now try making your own flow chart about getting dressed for school. Use these steps.

Start

Pick out shirt and slacks.

Do they match?

Change one of the items.

Put on the clothes.

Stop

Resources

Here are some books to help you teach your students how to start their own stamp collections:

A First Stamp Album for Beginners by Robert Obojski. Dover Publications, Inc., 1991.

Stamps by Mir Tamim. Rigby Education, 1997.

Stamp Collecting for Beginners by Burton H. Hobson. Wilshire Book Company, 1972.

These factual books tell about mail service:

A Day with a Mail Carrier by Jan Kottke. Children's Press, 2000.

Postal Workers Deliver Our Mail by Carol Greene. Child's World, Inc., 1998.

The Post Office Book: Mail & How It Moves by Gail Gibbons. HarperCollins, Inc., 1986.

A true story about a girl who was sent through the mail:

Mailing May by Michael O. Tunnell. William Morrow & Co., 2000.

Just for fun, here are some mail-related picture books:

The Jolly Postman by Allan Ahlberg. Little, Brown & Co., 1986.

Mail by the Pail by Colin Bergel. Wayne State University Press, 2000.

Never Mail an Elephant by Mike Thaler. Troll Communications, 1994.

No Mail for Mitchell by Catherine Siracusa. Random House, Inc., 1990.

Fire Prevention Week

Fire Prevention Week is held every year during either the first or second week of October. Get your students on the fire safety team by discussing this important topic together.

This is a great time to take a class trip to a nearby fire station. Or you may prefer to invite a fire fighter to visit your classroom. Also, be sure your students know the correct procedure in case of fire or a fire drill while they are at school. Also encourage them to talk with their families about fire safety in their homes.

Let students help you make the bulletin board display shown on page 150. Ask each student to trace a flame pattern on page 151 and to add a fire safety rule to the front of it. Sample rules can be found on page 152. Talk about the safety rules many times during Fire Prevention Week, and all year round.

Instruct your students to complete the skill-based reproducibles on the pages that follow. You will find a maze to solve, a picture to finish, plus several other language and math activities. You may notice that Dalmatians are referred to on several of the pages. These dogs are often associated with fire stations, and children find these dogs very appealing. Here are some interesting facts about Dalmatians which appear on the web site for National Fire Prevention Association at www.nfpa.org:

- Many years ago, Dalmatians were used to chase rats out of the fire stations and horse stables in London.

- Dalmatians are born with pure white coats. The spots appear as the dogs get older, and they are usually black or brown.

- During World War II, Dalmatians were used to carry secret messages and emergency supply kits.

- Dalmatians are "people dogs"; they love to spend time with their owners.

- They are extremely smart and may be easily bored.

- Dalmatians love to swim.

- George Washington and Benjamin Franklin owned Dalmatians.

- Dalmatians are also known as English Coach Dogs, Carriage Dogs and Plum Pudding Dogs.

Bulletin board
Fire Prevention Week

Never play with matches or lighters.

Remember to check the batteries in your smoke alarms.

Practice fire drills at home.

Have a plan of how to leave your house if it catches fire.

FIRE UP FOR SAFETY!

Be sure there is a smoke alarm near every bedroom.

Do not use fireworks. Let adults handle them.

Have a plan of where to meet your family in case of fire.

Be sure you know how to phone the fire department.

Fire prevention week begins October _____

Display this colorful bulletin board in time for Fire Prevention Week. Ask each student to trace the flame pattern found on page 151. Tell each child to write one safety rule on the front of the flame and his name on the back. Add each one to the bulletin board. See page 152 for possibie safety rules to include. You may wish to allow students to write safety rules of their own, even if they aren't directly related to fire prevention.

Background: white or light yellow
Logs: black or brown
Flames: red, orange and bright yellow

Safety Rules

These can be used with the bulletin board or
at anytime throughout the school year.

1. Never play with matches or lighters.

2. Anytime you see a fire, report it to an adult and phone 9-1-1.

3. If you are in a room that's on fire, crawl down on the floor to the nearest exit.

4. If your clothes catch on fire, stop moving, drop to the ground and roll around to put out the flames.

5. Do not use fireworks. Let adults handle them.

6. If you go to a fireworks display, stay a long distance away from where they are being lit.

7. Be sure there is a smoke alarm on every floor of your house.

8. Be sure there is a smoke alarm near every bedroom.

9. Remember to check the batteries in your smoke alarms.

10. Have a plan of how to leave your house if it catches fire.

11. Have a plan of where to meet your family in case of fire.

12. If your home has a fire, always leave the home. Then call 9-1-1 from a neighbor's house.

13. Practice fire drills at home.

14. Be sure you know how to phone the fire department.

15. Keep rags away from cans of gasoline.

16. Keep pot handles on the stove turned inward so they can't be bumped.

17. Keep potholders within easy reach of the stove.

18. Do not use electrical cords that are cracked or frayed.

Name _____

Make Way!

This fire truck needs to speed its way from the Fire Hall to the burning building.
Can you draw in a path the truck can follow?

Noting and drawing details
Truck Time

Look at these two fire trucks. Add the missing parts to the
truck on the bottom so that it looks just like the truck on top.

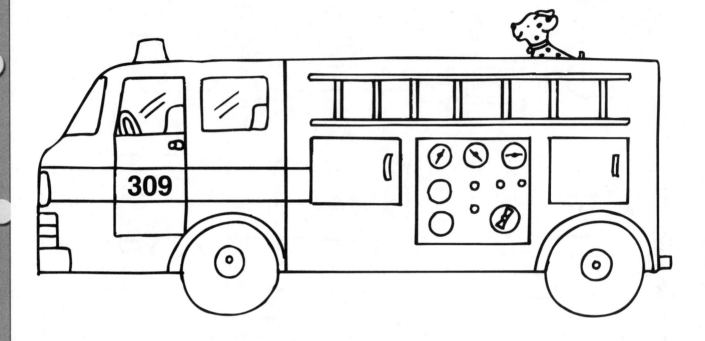

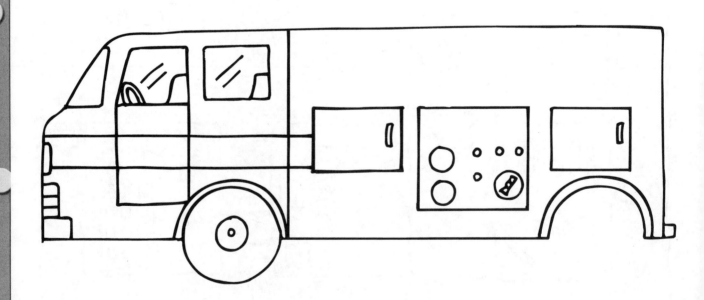

Name _____

Strike a Match

You know you should never play with matches, but you should try to find the matches on this page. Read the riddles. Each describes an object used in fighting or preventing fires. Draw a line to the correct name and picture for each one.

1. I'm like a giant faucet on the street. I can provide lots and lots of water from the city water supply to help fight a fire.

2. I'm a small, quiet item that hangs in your house. If there is a fire, though, I will make a lot of noise! Hopefully you have two or three of me in your home. Have you checked my batteries lately?

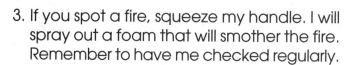

3. If you spot a fire, squeeze my handle. I will spray out a foam that will smother the fire. Remember to have me checked regularly.

4. I carry ladders, oxygen tanks, water pumps, hoses and more. Most importantly, I carry the fire fighters to the fire. If you see me coming down the street with flashing lights, please get out of my way!

Understanding sequence of events
Fighting Fires

Look at the pictures. They are in order to tell you a story. Read the sentences under the pictures. Write numbers to show the order in which things happened in the pictures.

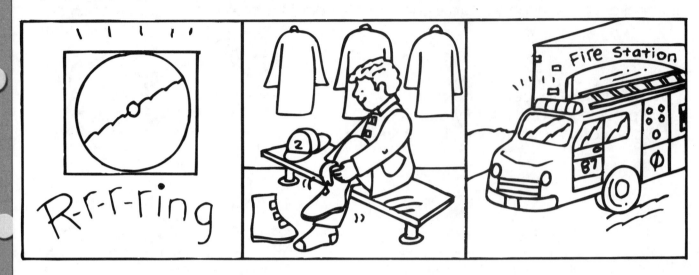

_____ The fire fighters put on their boots and hats.

_____ The fire alarm sounded.

_____ The fire truck drove to the fire.

_____ Fire fighters knew they must get ready to go to the fire.

_____ The Joneses put out their fire so it would not spread.

_____ The Joneses decided to go camping.

_____ The Joneses roasted hot dogs and marshmallows over their fire.

_____ The family carefully started a campfire.

Name _____

Dalmatians!

Fire fighters love to have Dalmatians. Can you count the number of dogs on this page? Do it this way: Circle a group of 10 dogs. Then circle another group of 10. Keep going until you run out of Dalmatians. How many sets of 10 did you circle? _____

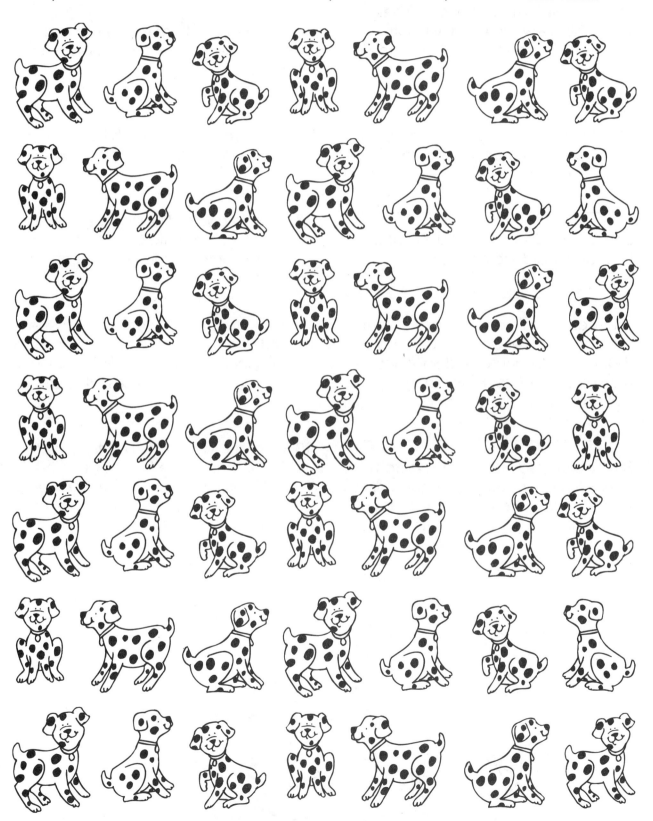

Solving word problems
Fire Fighters

Can you find the answers to these fire fighters' questions?
Write your answer in each blank.

1. The fire chief, Charlie, has 12 fire fighters on his crew. How many boots should there be for the 12 crew members?

_____

2. Charlie ordered 8 new fire hats. Only 3 were sent. How many more does he need?

_____

3. Sally phoned 9 of the 12 fire fighters. How many did she not call?

_____

4. There are 5 Dalmatians that live at the fire station. Chief Charlie has 2 more that live at his house and Sally has 1 more at her house. How many Dalmatians are there in all?

_____

5. Fire fighter Fred walks 3 blocks from his house to Fran's house. Fran then drives them 11 blocks to the Fire Hall. How many blocks in all does Fred travel?

_____

6. The 5 Dalmatians at the Fire Hall each have 2 ears. How many ears are there in all?

_____

7. The 5 Dalmatians each have 4 legs. How many legs are there in all?

_____

8. Charlie cooked hamburgers for supper. He ate 3, Sally ate 2 and Fred ate 3. How many burgers were eaten in all?

_____

9. One fire truck carries 3 hoses. One hose is 100 feet long. The second one is 60 feet long. The last one is 30 feet long. How long are the hoses altogether?

_____

10. All of the buttons fell off the chief's uniform. There were 5 buttons on the front of his uniform and 2 buttons on each sleeve. How many buttons need to be sewn on the uniform?

Columbus Day

On October 12, 1492, Christopher Columbus landed in North America. His voyage led to further exploration and the eventual settlement of the Americas. Columbus thought he had landed on an island off the coast of India, but was mistaken. At the time, no one knew the continents of North and South America even existed!

Celebrate the courage of Columbus during October as you commemorate Columbus Day. While the day used to be observed on October 12, since 1971 it has been recognized on the second Monday of the month.

Read "The Voyage of Christopher Columbus" on page 160 to your students. Then discuss with students these and similar questions:

• What new idea did Columbus have?

• Why did he want to go to Asia?

• What provisions did he need for the trip?

• Why did he need other crew members to go with him?

• What help did Columbus need from the king and queen of Spain?

• How do you know that Columbus was very brave?

• If you discovered a brand-new island, what would you name it?

Ask students to imagine what it would have been like to sail with Columbus on his adventure. Can they picture life aboard a sailing vessel? Can they imagine what it would have been like to live on the rations aboard, to encounter bad weather and to not really know where they were going? Ask students to pretend they were actually aboard the *Santa Maria* with Columbus and had kept a journal. Instruct students to write imaginary diary pages and keep them inside a book, using the shape book pattern on page 168. (Alternatively, you may ask students to write facts about Columbus in their shape books.)

Make Columbus Day edible sailing ships. Use stalks of celery, cut in lengths of about four inches, as "boats." Fill the bottom of the boats with cheese spread, cream cheese or peanut butter. Stand up pretzel sticks in the filling as masts. Complete the ships by adding "sails" of large marshmallows or cubes of cheese or bread.

Use a globe to demonstrate the route taken by Columbus. Talk about his idea of traveling east to go west. Tell students that at the time of his journey, Columbus and the rest of the world did not know that North America lay between Europe and Asia. You will also find the map activity on page 167 to be helpful.

On the pages that follow, you will also find a variety of language activities for students to complete. Students can practice some simple math concepts, too. So set your sail for an educational Columbus Day!

Name _____

The Voyage of Christopher Columbus

Read this article aloud to your students. Then distribute copies of page 161.

In 1492, Christopher Columbus set off on a daring voyage. He was in command of three ships, the *Niña*, the *Pinta* and the *Santa Maria*. He took with him crews for every ship plus food, supplies and an empty chest in which to store treasure that he hoped to find on the trip.

The purpose of Columbus's trip was to find a new sea route to Asia. Other explorers only sailed east from Europe. But Columbus believed that if he sailed west he could reach India more quickly. He did not know that he would first find the Americas. The map he used did not show North and South America, Australia or even the Pacific Ocean.

He set sail in August, and two months later, in October, he sighted land which he believed was Asia. In fact, Columbus had arrived at some islands near Florida. He did not realize what he had found, but his journey paved the way for other travelers to explore and settle the Americas.

Instruct students to look at the handout (page 161). Give them these directions:

1. Write your name at the top of the page.

2. Do you remember from the story how many boats went on the voyage with Columbus? Draw in more smaller boats so that you have the correct number.

3. Look at the compass. In which direction did Columbus want to sail? Circle that word.

4. The ships relied on wind power. Draw sails on each of your ships.

5. The largest ship, the *Santa Maria*, had a crew of 40 people. Write the number 40 inside one of the sails on your largest ship.

6. Crew members had to sleep on the ships. Notice the bunkbeds in the first ship. Draw stick figures of people sleeping in the bunks.

7. The crew needed food. Draw crates of food inside all of your ships.

8. Do you remember how many months Columbus traveled before reaching land? Write the number of months next to your name.

The Voyage of Christopher Columbus

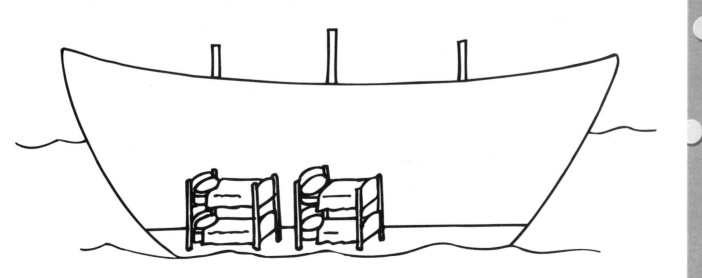

Capitalizing proper nouns
Capital Idea!

When Christopher Columbus decided to try sailing east to travel west, this was a brand-new idea. Read these sentences that tell more about his idea. Remember that proper nouns, or nouns that name a certain person, place or thing must begin with a capital letter. Circle each word below that is a proper noun.
Write only the proper nouns on the blanks, and begin each one with a capital letter.

1. Christopher columbus was born in genoa, italy.

   _____

2. Genoa was one of the busiest trading ports in europe.

   _____

3. In genoa, jewels, spices, silks and ivories came from india and china.

   _____

4. These goods had traveled over both land and sea, ending with a route through the mediterranean sea.

   _____

5. All countries in europe wanted to find an all-water route to india.

   _____

6. When christopher columbus decided to make his voyage, he asked the king of portugal to help pay for the trip.

   _____

7. When the king of portugal refused, columbus asked the king and queen of spain.

   _____

8. King ferdinand and queen isabella of spain were interested in helping columbus.

   _____

9. Columbus finally set sail in august of 1492, taking three ships: the *niña*, the *pinta*, and the *santa maria*.

   _____

10. On october 12, 1492, columbus reached the small island of san salvador in north america.

   _____

Name _____

Sailing Search

Surely Columbus must have needed to search for a lot of things before he began his famous voyage in 1492. Now it's your turn to search for many words related to that trip. Look across, down and diagonally in the sail to find words. The word list is in the boat.

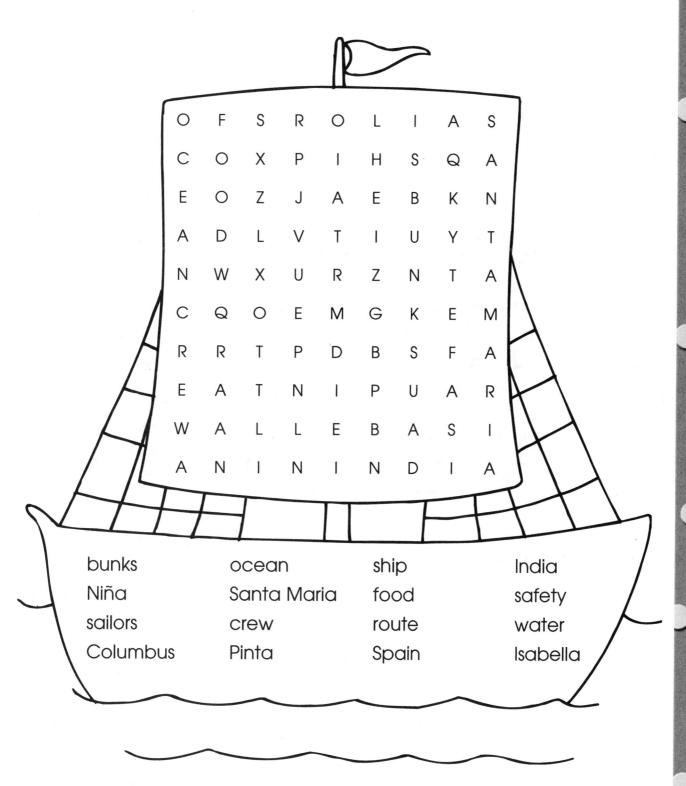

```
O  F  S  R  O  L  I  A  S
C  O  X  P  I  H  S  Q  A
E  O  Z  J  A  E  B  K  N
A  D  L  V  T  I  U  Y  T
N  W  X  U  R  Z  N  T  A
C  Q  O  E  M  G  K  E  M
R  R  T  P  D  B  S  F  A
E  A  T  N  I  P  U  A  R
W  A  L  L  E  B  A  S  I
A  N  I  N  I  N  D  I  A
```

bunks	ocean	ship	India
Niña	Santa Maria	food	safety
sailors	crew	route	water
Columbus	Pinta	Spain	Isabella

Ordinal numbers
Count for Columbus

Look for the circled object in each row.
Write the correct ordinal number on the line from the words below.
Color all of the objects.

| first | second | third | fourth | fifth |
| sixth | seventh | eigth | ninth | tenth |

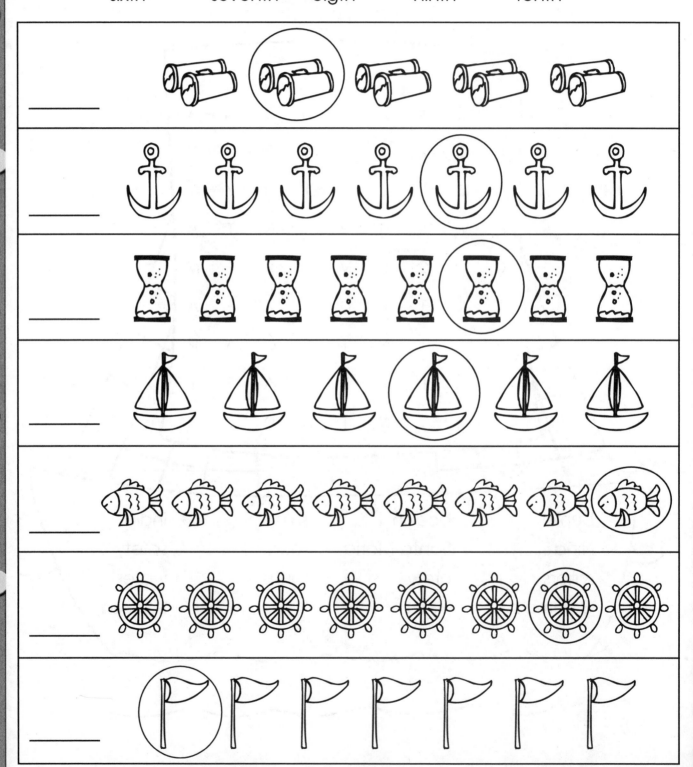

Name _____

Tall or Small?

Circle the tallest person or object. Color the shortest.

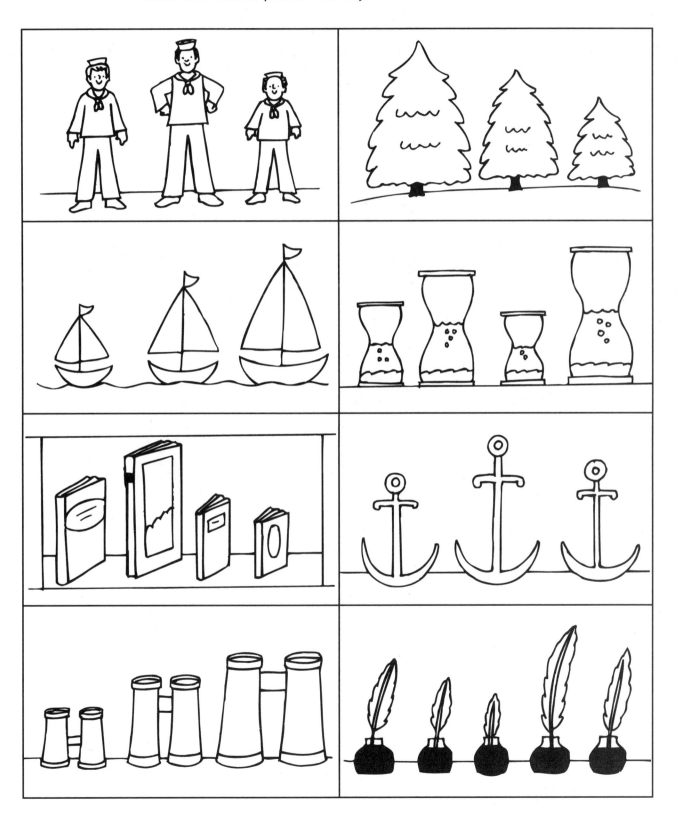

Name _____

Subtraction of multiple numbers

Race Pace

Which of the three ships will reach the finish line first? Subtract to find out. Each ship begins with 99 points. But the racers want to get rid of the points. Keep subtracting the numbers in each lane, one at a time. The runner with the lowest number of points wins. Write the number of points for each ship at the end of the race. Circle the boat that wins.

Santa Maria	Niña	Pinta
99	99	99
− 13	− 20	− 32
− 25	− 3	− 4
− 6	− 32	− 13
−10	−16	−20
− 31	− 18	− 15

Totals: _____   _____   _____

Finish

Teacher: Help your students complete this page. If possible, reproduce map on an overhead transparency, and work through each step of the instructions with students.

The Voyage of Columbus

Use this map to learn about the first voyage of Christopher Columbus.

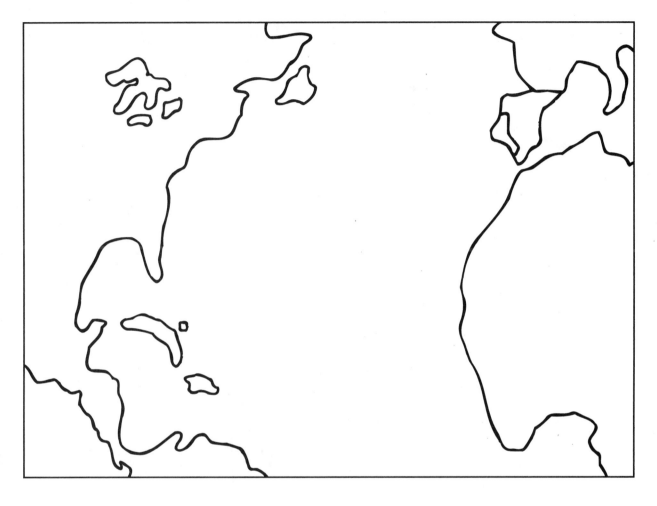

1. Label north, south, east and west in the correct places around the edges of the map.

2. Label the Atlantic Ocean. Color it blue.

3. Label Europe. Color it green.

4. Label North America. Color it purple.

5. Find the location of Spain. Label it with S. This is where his trip began.

6. Find the location of San Salvador. This is where Columbus landed. Label this tiny island with SS.

7. Draw a line from Spain to San Salvador. This line shows (in general) the journey taken by Columbus.

Shape Book Pattern

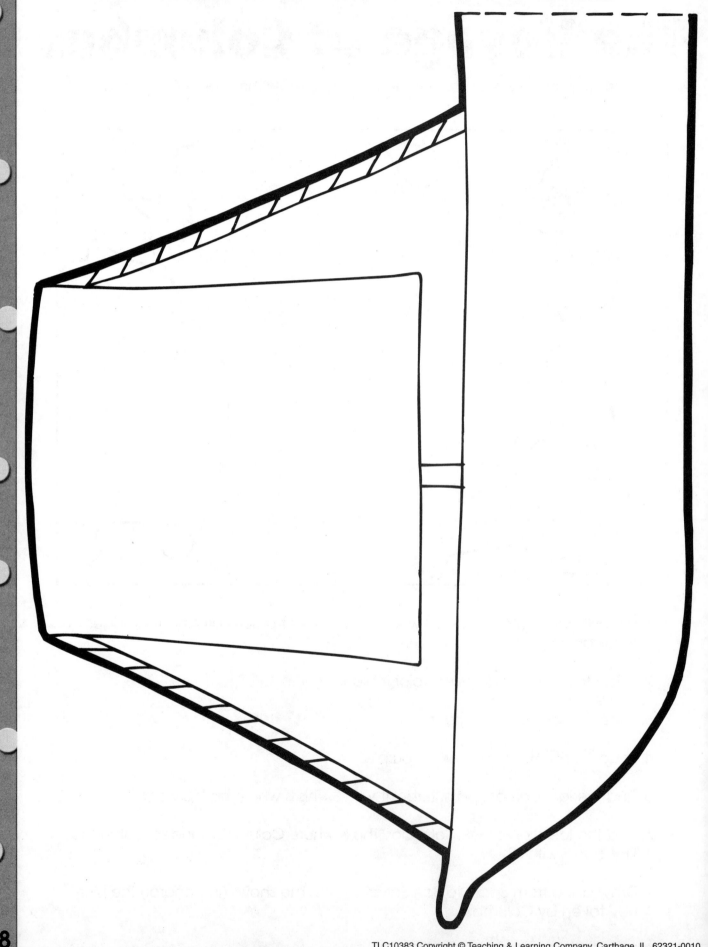

Resources

Picture Books and Biographies Suitable for Children Ages 4-8

Christopher Columbus: (Step into Reading Book Series: A Step 2 Book) by Stephen Krensky. Random House, Inc., 1999.

Christopher Columbus and His Voyage to America by Robert Young. Silver Burdett Press, 1990.

Columbus Day by Vicki Liestman. The Lerner Publishing Group, 1992.

In Fourteen Ninety-Two by Jean Marzollo. Scholastic, Inc., 1993. (This book has rhyming text.)

Meet Christopher Columbus by James Tertiums DeKay. Random House, Inc., 1989.

Picture Book of Christopher Columbus by David A. Adler, et al. Holiday House, Inc., 1991. (Note: This book is available with a cassette tape from Live Oak Media, 1992.)

The Story of Columbus by Anita Ganeri. Dorling Kindersley Publishing, 2001.

Young Christopher Columbus: Discoverer of New Worlds (First-Step Biographies) by Eric Carpenter. Troll Assoc., 1992.

Book for Older Readers (but young ones may relish the photographs and illustrations)

DK Discoveries: Christopher Columbus: Explorer of the New World by Peter Chrisp. Dorling Kindersley Publishing, 2001. For ages 9-12.

Teacher Resource Books

Draw, Write, Now—Book 2: Christopher Columbus, Autumn Harvest, Weather by Marie Hablitzel and Kin H. Stitzer. Barker Creek Publishing, Inc., 1995. A collection of drawing and handwriting lessons for ages 5-10.

History—Hands On! Christopher Columbus by Mary Tucker. Teaching & Learning Company, 2002. Activities and reproducibles for grades 1-4.

Dictionary Day

Dictionary Day is held on October 16 to honor Noah Webster who was born on this day in 1758. Webster authored the first American dictionaries of the English language.

Invite your students into the wonderful words that await them inside a dictionary. In spare minutes throughout the week, or in a block of time all at once, present some of these challenges to your young scholars. Use a set of classroom dictionaries, if possible, so all are using the same edition.

Mystery Word

Start the game by selecting a word that is familiar, or somewhat familiar, to the class, such as *drop*. Give clues to your word, while students flip through their dictionaries in search of it. Here are sample clues for *drop*: 1. My word starts with D. 2. It has four letters. 3. It starts with DR. 4. It has (six) different meanings. 5. One of the meanings is "a small amount of liquid" and so on. The first child to correctly guess the word gets to select the next mystery word in his dictionary and to make up the clues.

Scavenger Hunt

Call out general descriptions of words, one at a time. You might ask students to find a word with a double Z, for example. The first one to find one (such as *fuzzy*) gets a sticker or a small treat. Another option is to write the category on the board at the beginning of the day and award a prize to the person who can find the most words in that category by the end of the day. Categories will vary by the level of the students, but here are some other possible topics:

- four-letter J words
- words that end in *AL*
- words that have a *Q* anywhere except the first letter
- words with more than three definitions
- nouns that begin with K
- words with more than three syllables
- words that can be both nouns and verbs

Speed Drill

Be sure all students have a dictionary. Call out a word that is unknown to most students. Try to choose words that may be new, but will have meaning and relevance for the children. The first child to find the word stands up and reads its first definition. You may award points or stickers as well. Keep track of the new words on the chalkboard. Try to use the words in other activities throughout the week. Sample words to use: *drone, epic, guzzle, kumquat, mosaic* and *poise*.

ABC order-first letter
Dictionary Duty

Can you put these words in order, as they would appear in a dictionary? Number each group of words from 1 to 5 to show which comes first, second and so on.

A
_____ tiger
_____ lion
_____ cougar
_____ panther
_____ bobcat

B
_____ shirt
_____ apron
_____ coat
_____ blouse
_____ tie

C
_____ squash
_____ corn
_____ peas
_____ radishes
_____ beets

D
_____ Val
_____ Mel
_____ Fred
_____ Wes
_____ Pam

E
_____ soccer
_____ hockey
_____ baseball
_____ football
_____ tennis

F
_____ red
_____ yellow
_____ pink
_____ green
_____ orange

G
_____ one
_____ six
_____ eight
_____ four
_____ nine

H
_____ huge
_____ big
_____ large
_____ great
_____ enormous

I
_____ bus
_____ car
_____ ship
_____ truck
_____ jeep

ABC order-second letter
123, ABC

Little Webster, Junior wants to put these words in the right order. But each set of three words begins with the same letter! He needs to look at the second letter, then, to know how to place the words. Write the words in the blanks to show the right order.

Example: dish   1. desk   2. dish   3. dust
            desk
            dust

A. best   1. _____   2. _____   3. _____
    bread
    bake

B. fudge   1. _____   2. _____   3. _____
    fine
    freeze

C. help   1. _____   2. _____   3. _____
    hand
    hip

D. judge   1. _____   2. _____   3. _____
    jelly
    jam

E. zip   1. _____   2. _____   3. _____
    zone
    zap

F. prize   1. _____   2. _____   3. _____
    pest
    pump

G. gas   1. _____   2. _____   3. _____
    guess
    grease

H. toy   1. _____   2. _____   3. _____
    trick
    tack

Halloween

Let all of your students help fill this Halloween bulletin board. Talk about words that rhyme with the four words placed on the the board. Instruct students to cut out a matching shape, label it with a word that rhymes and add it to the display. For example, Susie might cut out a bat, label it with *hat* and add it to the "bat" area of the board. Sammy might cut out a mask, label it with *ask* and add it to that portion of the board. See the four patterns on page 174.

Shape Book Pattern

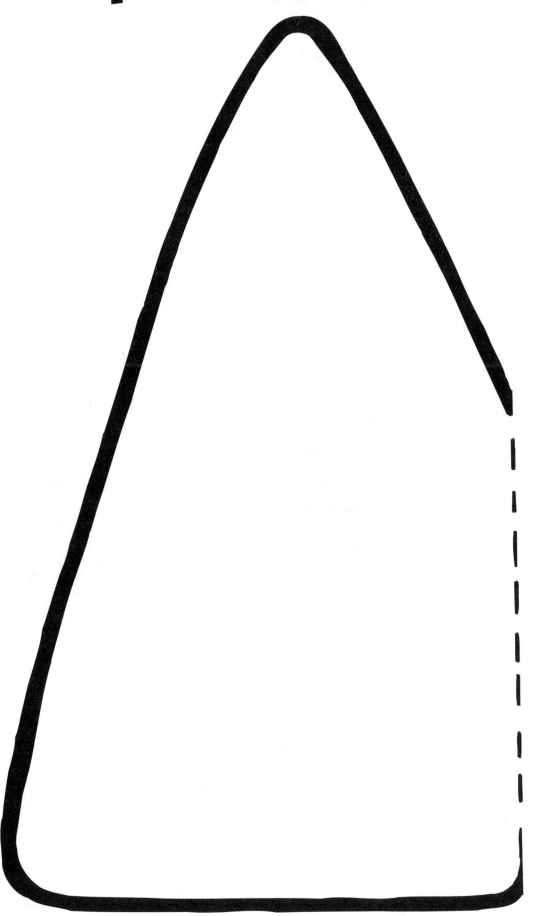

Teacher: *Distribute copies of this poem to read aloud with your students.*
They may like to make up actions to go with the poem. They may color the picture.

Trick-or-Treat

Trick-or-treat,
It's time to eat
All the good snacks
That were put in my sack:
Apples and raisins and candy corn,
Chocolates and peanuts and even popcorn.
Lots of sweets
And tasty treats
I'll share with my mother,
My sister, my brother.
And just for Dad,
I have to add,
There's a big candy bar
In the shape of his car!

Name _____

*Teacher: Photocopy this page and the next, mount them on tagboard
and then laminate. (You may ask students to color them before laminating.)*

Halloween Hunt

Grab a friend and head to the Halloween party! Play with two, three or four people in all.
Use a different marker for each player. Begin on Start and take turns rolling a die.
Move around the board and follow the directions on the space where you land.
The first player to Finish wins.

Start

Move ahead to the next pumpkin.

Yuck!
You're stuck in a cob web. Lose your next turn.

If you can name 5 words that rhyme with *bat*, move ahead 2 spaces.

Good job!
You shared your Halloween candy. Take an extra turn.

Oops!
You ate too much candy and must go see the dentst. Lose your next turn.

Happy ○ Halloween

Oooh! You've stepped in a glob of bubble gum. Lose your next turn.

If you can name 3 words that rhyme with *treat* move ahead to Finish.

Finish

If you can tell the date of Halloween this year, move ahead 3 spaces.

You won first place for your costume. Congratulations! Move ahead 1 space.

You invited a friend to go to the party with you. Move ahead 2 spaces.

Name _____

Halloween Surprise

Use this story with the questions on page 180.

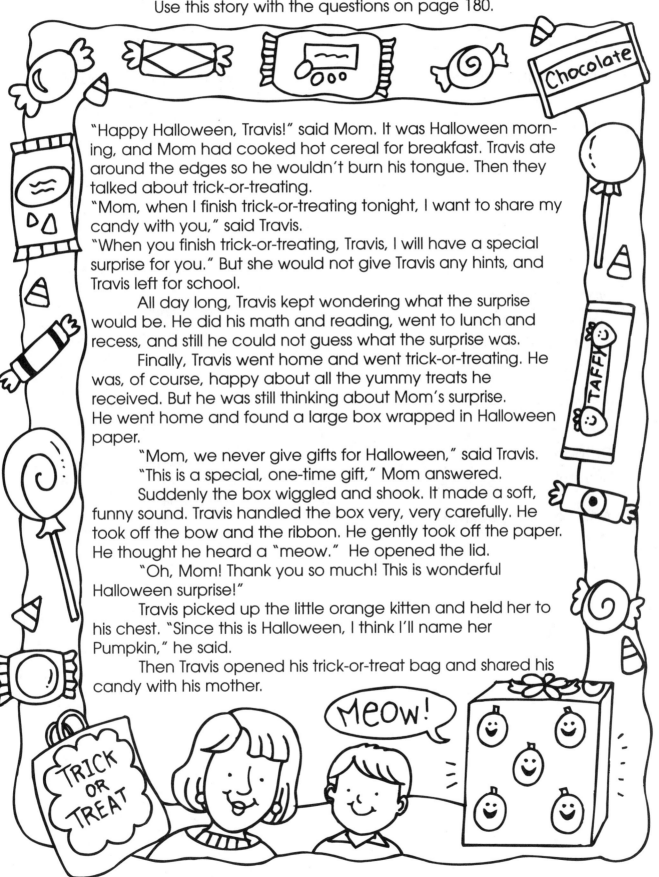

"Happy Halloween, Travis!" said Mom. It was Halloween morning, and Mom had cooked hot cereal for breakfast. Travis ate around the edges so he wouldn't burn his tongue. Then they talked about trick-or-treating.

"Mom, when I finish trick-or-treating tonight, I want to share my candy with you," said Travis.

"When you finish trick-or-treating, Travis, I will have a special surprise for you." But she would not give Travis any hints, and Travis left for school.

All day long, Travis kept wondering what the surprise would be. He did his math and reading, went to lunch and recess, and still he could not guess what the surprise was.

Finally, Travis went home and went trick-or-treating. He was, of course, happy about all the yummy treats he received. But he was still thinking about Mom's surprise. He went home and found a large box wrapped in Halloween paper.

"Mom, we never give gifts for Halloween," said Travis.

"This is a special, one-time gift," Mom answered.

Suddenly the box wiggled and shook. It made a soft, funny sound. Travis handled the box very, very carefully. He took off the bow and the ribbon. He gently took off the paper. He thought he heard a "meow." He opened the lid.

"Oh, Mom! Thank you so much! This is wonderful Halloween surprise!"

Travis picked up the little orange kitten and held her to his chest. "Since this is Halloween, I think I'll name her Pumpkin," he said.

Then Travis opened his trick-or-treat bag and shared his candy with his mother.

Meow!

Name _____

Halloween Surprise

Read the story called "Halloween Surprise."
Then answer these questions. Circle the right answers.

1. What was the surprise?
   an orange kitten
   a black puppy
   a white kitten

2. How was the surprise gift wrapped?
   in a bag
   in a box, with paper and ribbon
   in an envelope

3. What did Travis eat for breakfast?
   bacon and eggs
   cornflakes
   hot cereal

4. What month was it?
   September
   October
   November

5. Who cooked breakfast?
   Mom
   Dad
   Travis

6. When did Travis go trick-or-treating?
   before school
   after school
   after he opened the surprise gift

7. From this story, how do you know that Mom cares about Travis? (Circle all the right answers.)
   she cooked his breakfast
   she ate some of his candy
   she took him to school
   she gave him a gift

8. From this story, how do you know that Travis uses good manners? (Circle all the right answers.)
   he raised his hand in class
   he thanked his mom for the gift
   he covered his mouth when he sneezed
   he shared his candy with his mom

9. Just for fun, if you were given an orange kitten on Halloween, what would you name it?

   _____

Name _____

Tricky Letters

Trick and *treat* both start with the consonant blend TR.
Can you sound out the word for each picture?
Circle the consonant blend that your hear at the beginning of each word.

sl sk sp	fr fl gr	ch cl cr
sl sp st	sl sw sk	bl cl gl
fl cl bl	cl fl pl	sc sl st

Addition with money

Monster Munchies

Max dressed up like a monster to go to a Halloween party at the mall.
Now he is as hungry as a big monster! He has all the coins
shown on this page. He wants to buy one of each of the snacks shown below.

Cut out the coins. Find a way to use all of the coins to buy
one of each treat shown. Paste the coins into the right
places.

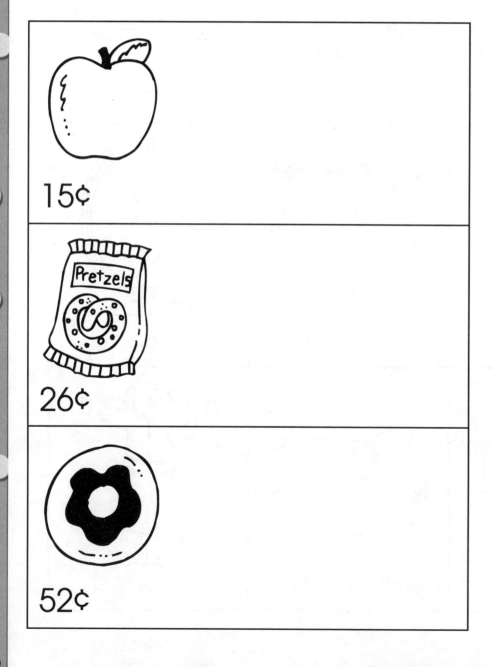

15¢

26¢

52¢

Name _____

Third Try

Here is a Halloween treat that has three equal parts, or thirds. Each part equals 1/3. If you and two of your friends each had one piece, you would all have the same amount of the treat.

Look at these shapes. If the shape shows thirds (three equal parts), circle it. If does not show thirds, put an X on it.

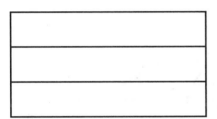
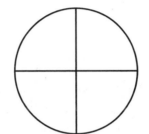
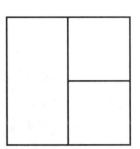

Color 1/3 of the pie.

Color 2/3 of the square.

Color 2/3 of these jack-o'-lanterns.

Bookmarks

Use these bookmarks during the special days in October.

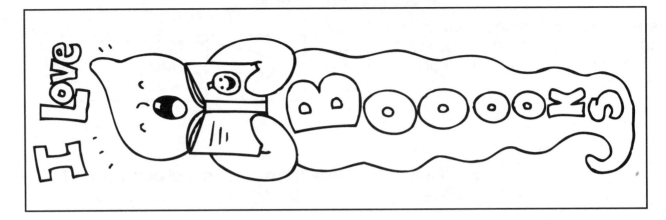

November

Get ready for nifty November with a fresh assortment of bulletin boards, teacher helps and curriculum reproducible pages to see you through many of the special days in November.

We've chosen six special themes for this month: National American Indian Heritage Month, the White House, Sandwich Day, World Kindness Week, National Children's Book Week and, of course, Thanksgiving. For some of these themes you will find bulletin boards, snack ideas and resource lists. For others you might see a song, a student game idea or a poem. For *all* of the units you will have appealing reproducibles that cover autumn skills in math, language arts and more.

Simply pick the themes you are most interested in and select activities and worksheets that are on an appropriate level for your students. You will be able to use many ideas in each unit even though some individual pages may be too difficult or too simple for your particular class.

First your students will observe National American Indian Heritage Month. On these pages you'll find a shape book and a bulletin board idea, complete with patterns and language activities. Reproducibles help students practice counting shapes, complete addition sentences and more. You'll also find a list of helpful resources.

November 1 marks the anniversary of the President occupying the White House. Take your students on a tour of the White House grounds through a listening lesson in the second section of this month. Learn about its history in a sequencing page. Teach the proper form for writing a letter as students pen a note to the President.

Kids love sandwiches, and we've included some unusual, but delicious, variations on the popular peanut butter sandwich. Students can solve a cut-and-paste puzzle and read a poem aloud with their classmates. ABC order, logic and subtraction are also covered.

World Kindness Week deserves special notice, and these activities will help your students focus on being *nice* to each other. National Children's Book Week is a great time to play a game that matches authors with their books. You'll find a circular book report and a patterned writing activity. Don't miss the "fishy" bulletin board here!

Finally, celebrate Thanksgiving with a pre-holiday party. You'll find suggestions on the teacher page at the last of the month. Also included are a shape book, a visual discrimination activity and language and math reproducibles.

Don't forget all the great clip art on the CD. It promises to make for a truly nifty November in *your* classroom!

National American Indian Heritage Month

By presidential proclamation, November is known as National American Indian Heritage Month. Enjoy our rich history as you lead your students through the activities on the pages that follow. A bulletin board idea and patterns are shown on pages 188-190. Don't miss the resources listed on page 198.

If possible, plan a trip to a museum that features an exhibit of Native American art or history. Or invite a local resident of Native American heritage to share stories from his family's oral history. Check your own house for Native American crafts and jewelry items that you can bring to class to share with your students.

A drawing of a woven mat for students to color is shown on page 197. You may also want your students to try a little weaving for themselves.

- Begin with a 9" x 12" piece of construction paper. Fold it in half, then cut slots in the page about 1" apart, as shown at the right. Stop cutting about 1" before you reach the edge of the paper.

- Cut strips of a contrasting color, measuring about 3/4" x 9". Weave these strips through the slots on the first paper. Tape both ends of the strips to the back of the mat. Tell students to start the first strip going over, under, over, under and the second strip going under, over, under, over to get the best results.

Corn was a favorite crop and food of many Native American tribes. Corn and its many products are also very popular foods today. Try one of these easy snacks as you observe National American Indian Heritage Month this November:

- Bake corn muffins made from a purchased cornbread mix. Students can read and follow directions to add milk, eggs and oil, and then to bake the muffins in the oven. CAUTION! Be sure an adult places muffin pans in and out of the oven. Serve the warm muffins with margarine and/or honey, if desired.

- Make individual servings of tortillas and cheese. Purchase a bag of white or yellow corn chips and some shredded mozzarella or cheddar cheese. Ask each student to arrange 6-8 chips in the center of a microwavable plate and top with cheese. Microwave on high power for just 10-15 seconds, until the cheese melts. Kids can eat the chips and melted cheese with their fingers!

- Don't forget popcorn!

fold

National American Indian Heritage Month

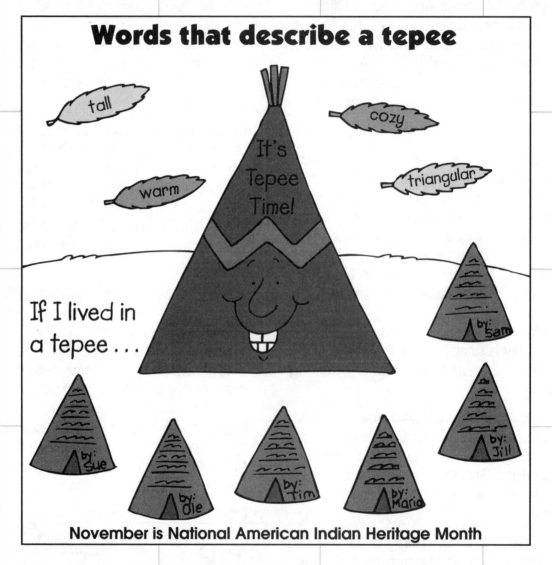

Words that describe a tepee

tall

cozy

warm

triangular

It's Tepee Time!

If I lived in a tepee . . .

by: Sam

by: Sue

by: Ole

by: Tim

by: Maria

by: Jill

November is National American Indian Heritage Month

For the top of the display, students should list adjectives to describe a tepee. Ask them to try to imagine what a tepee would look like, how it would feel and how it would smell. They may write their words on a feather and add it to the display. For the bottom of the bulletin board, ask students to finish the sentence. They may write their responses on a miniature tepee and add it to the bulletin board. See page 189-190 for patterns.

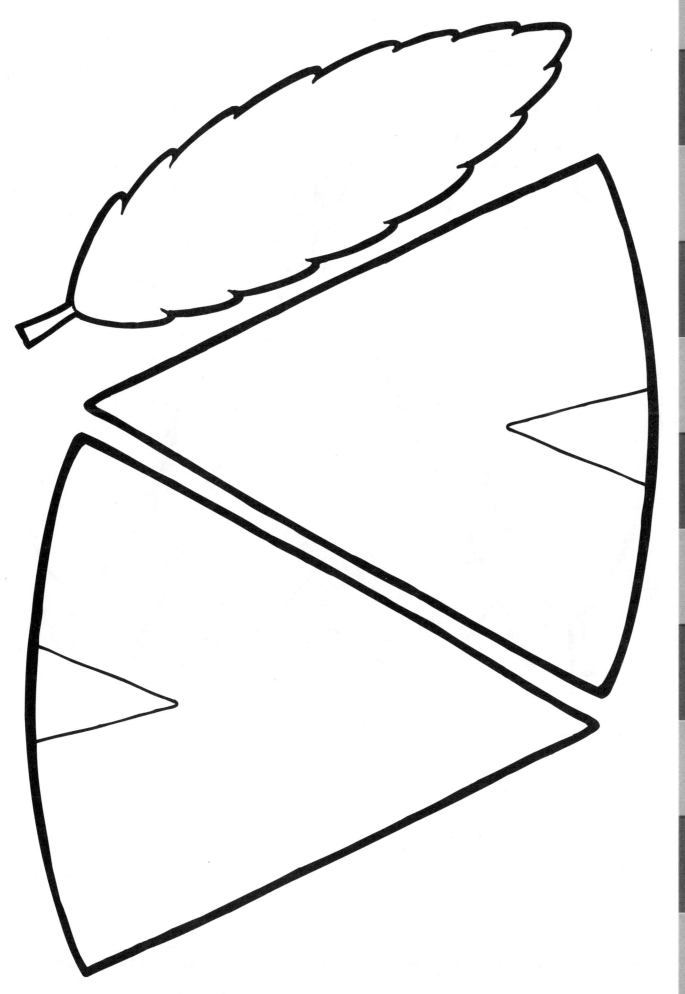

Shape Book Pattern

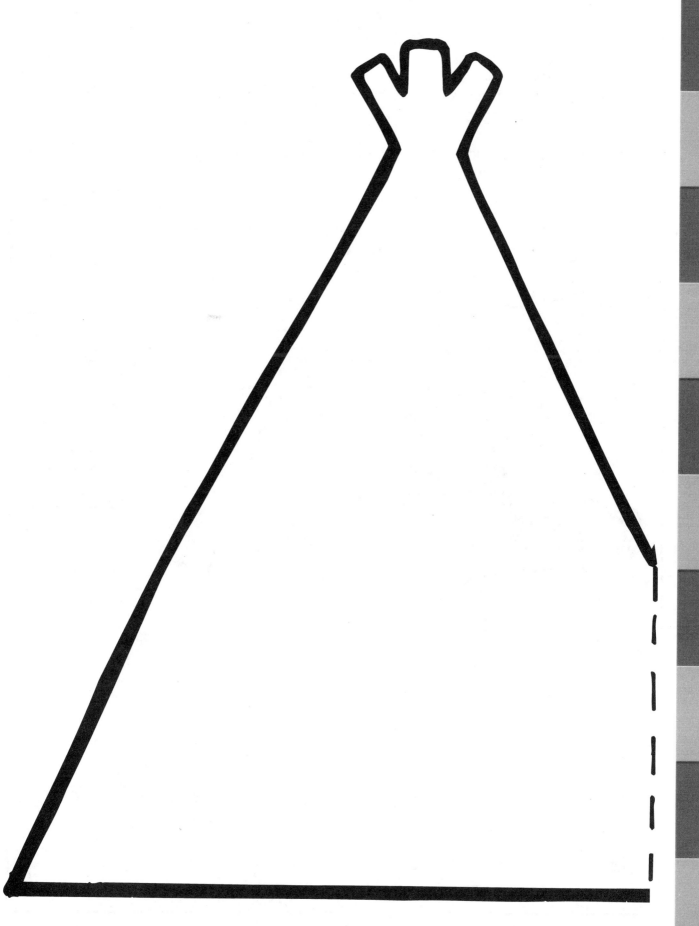

Identifying and counting triangles

Tepees

Tribes of Native Americans on the Great Plains, including the Sioux tribe and others, lived in tepees. Tepees were made of buffalo hides stretched over a wooden frame and were easy to put up. A fire was lit inside the tepee for cooking and warmth. Flaps at the top of the tepee could be opened to let smoke escape.

From a distance, tepees looked like triangles dotting the plains. Look at the picture and color all the triangles that you see. How many did you count? _____

Final long e sound

Tepee Ends in E!

Say the word *tepee*, and listen for the long *e* sound at the end of the word. Do you know other words that end in the long *e* sound? Sometimes the sound is spelled with other letters in addition to, or instead of, the letter *e*. Some examples are *sea* and *monkey*. Look at the words below. If you hear the long *e* sound at the *end* of the word, color the picture. If you don't hear the long *e* sound, put an X on the picture.

key

zebra

tree

puppy

broccoli

bee

horse

fly

turkey

chimney

canoe

flea

Reading comprehension
Tepee Time

A brave and his father are putting up a tepee.
Read each sentence. Draw a line to the picture that matches it.

1. First, we make long poles from trees. Then we put up the poles. We bind them together at the top to make a cone shape.

2. Next we stretch buffalo hides over the frame. We use lodge pins made from bone to hold the hides together. We also use pins at the bottom of the tepee to hold it down against the ground.

3. Finally we cut a door flap and decorate the tepee with story pictures.

Name _____

Many words that we use came from Native American words. A few them are hidden in the tepee below. Look across, up, down and diagonally to find the words in the puzzle.

Alaska	avocado	canoe	chili	hickory	opossum
llama	Mississippi	moose	Nebraska	Oklahoma	iguana
skunk	Texas	tamale	guava	hurricane	potato

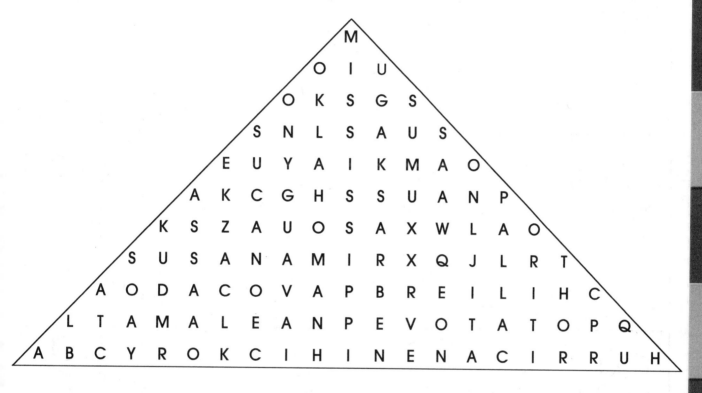

```
                    M
                  O   I   U
                O   K   S   G   S
              S   N   L   S   A   U   S
            E   U   Y   A   I   K   M   A   O
          A   K   C   G   H   S   S   U   A   N   P
        K   S   Z   A   U   O   S   A   X   W   L   A   O
      S   U   S   A   N   A   M   I   R   X   Q   J   L   R   T
    A   O   D   A   C   O   V   A   P   B   R   E   I   L   I   H   C
  L   T   A   M   A   L   E   A   N   P   E   V   O   T   A   T   O   P   Q
A   B   C   Y   R   O   K   C   I   H   I   N   E   N   A   C   I   R   R   U   H
```

1. Which words are animals? _____ _____

_____ _____ _____

2. Which words are things you can eat? _____ _____

_____ _____ _____

3. Which word do you think comes from the Indian words meaning "big waters"?

_____

4. Which words are names of states in the U.S.A.? _____

_____ _____ _____

Addition
Count the Corn

We have Native Americans to thank for one of our favorite snacks—popcorn!
Count the kernels of popcorn below. Draw more kernels and write
a number so that the math sentence is right.

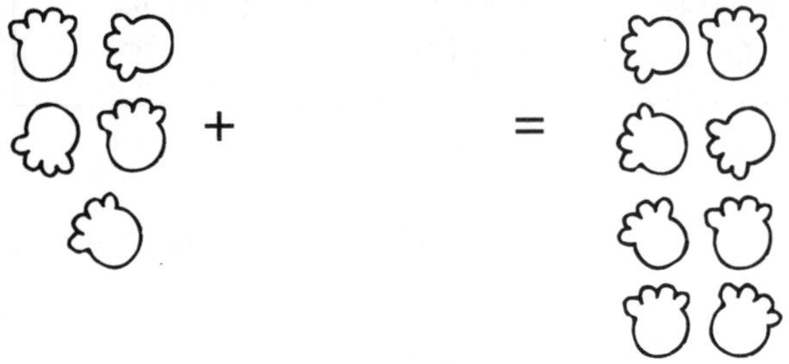

$5 +$ _____ $= 8$

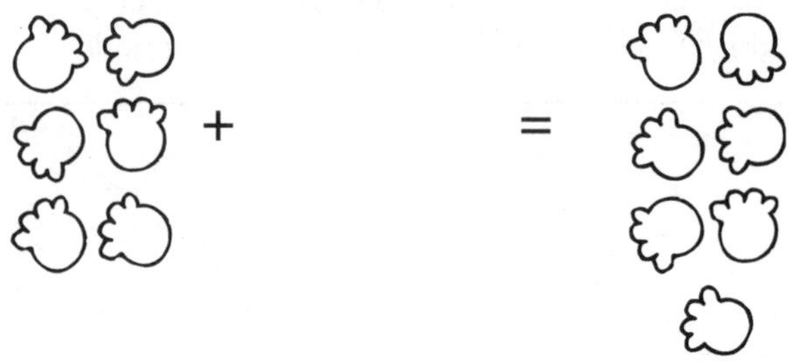

$6 +$ _____ $= 7$

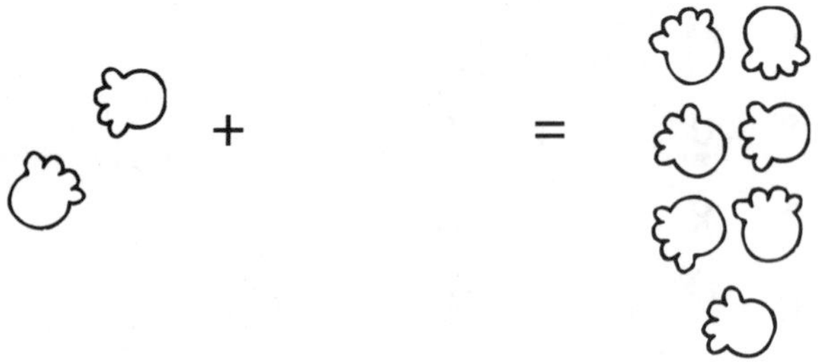

$2 +$ _____ $= 7$

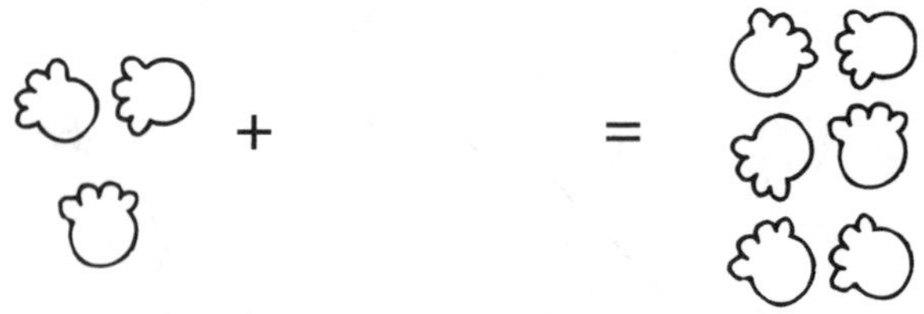

$3 +$ _____ $= 6$

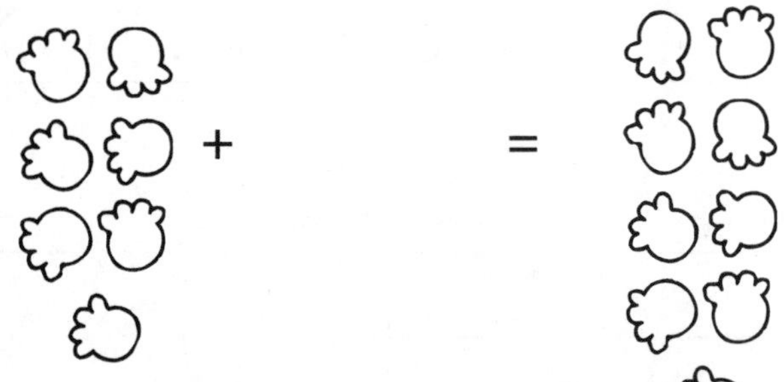

$7 +$ _____ $= 9$

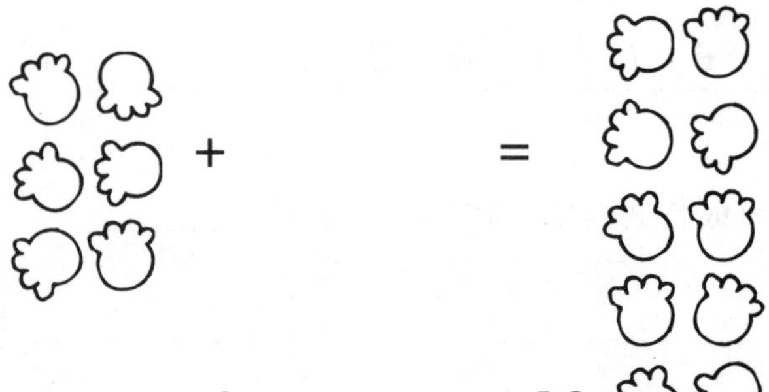

$6 +$ _____ $= 10$

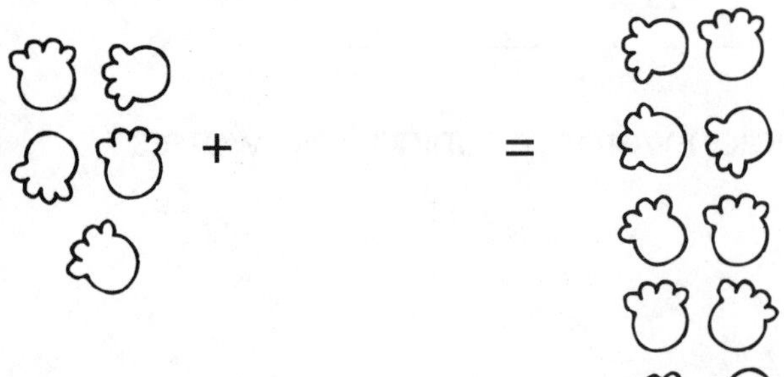

$5 +$ _____ $= 10$

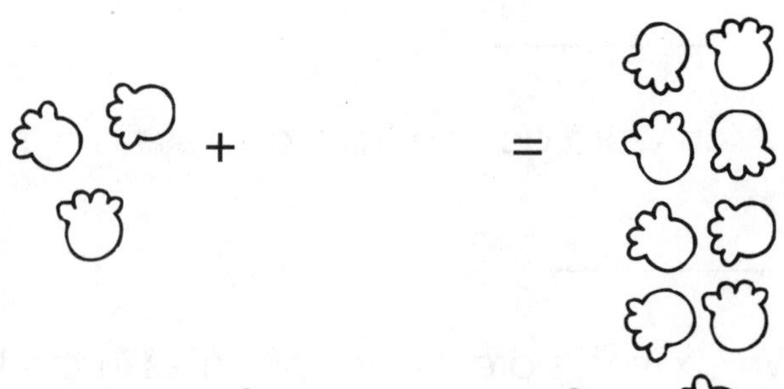

$3 +$ _____ $= 9$

Name _____

Color by number

Native American Crafts

Native Americans have a history of making beautiful woven fabrics and pottery.
Use the chart to color the two examples shown.

1 = green
2 = red
3 = blue
4 = yellow
5 = black
6 = brown
7 = orange

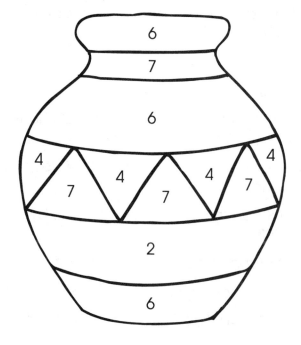

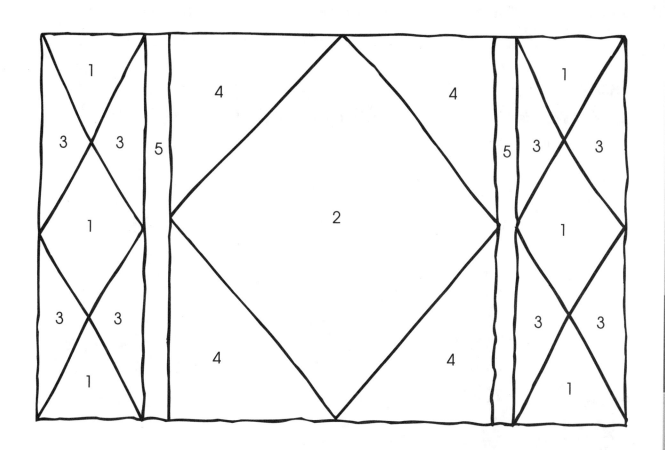

Resources

Non-Fiction

Concise Encyclopedia of the American Indian by Bruce Grant and Lorence F. Bjorklund. Random House Value Publishing, Inc., 1989.

Courage of Sarah Noble by Alice Dalgliesh. Simon & Schuster, 1986.

Corn Is Maize: The Gift of the Indians by Aliki. HarperCollins Children's Books, 1996.

Fiction, Folklore and Legends

Arrow to the Sun: A Pueblo Indian Tale illustrated by Gerald McDermott. Penguin U.S.A., 1977.

Buffalo Before Breakfast (Magic Tree House Series #18) by Mary Pope Ozborne, Random House, Inc., 1999.

Coyote Steals the Blanket: An Ute Tale by Janet Stevens. Holiday House, Inc., 1993.

The Gift of the Sacred Dog by Paul Goble. Macmillan Publishing, 1984.

The Girl Who Loved Wild Horses by Paul Goble. Simon & Schuster, 1986.

Knots on a Counting Rope by Bill Martin, et al. Henry Holt and Company, Inc., 1997.

Sootface: An Ojibwa Cinderella Story by Robert D. San Souci. Dell Publishing Co., Inc., 1997

VHS/DVD

Tales of Wonder: Traditional Native American Stories for Children (1998)

Volume I: UPC 669910606230

Volume II: UPC 652645652948

The White House

November marks the anniversary of the President of the United States moving into the White House. On November 1, 1800, President John Adams and his family moved into the newly completed White House in Washington, D.C. Every subsequent President has also lived there. So George Washington has the distinction of being the only President who did *not* live in the White House. The White House is one of the most popular tourist spots in the country. Over one million people visit it each year.

November, then, is a great time for your students to learn more about the home of the leader of the United States and its history. The listening lesson in this unit (see pages 200-201) will supply your students with some basic information about the structure as they launch into this fascinating topic.

Here are additional activities for your students:

• Ask students to think about what it would be like if they were moving into the White House. Play this memory game. The first child says, "I'm moving into the White House, and I'm taking an aquarium (or other *a* word)." The second child says, "I'm moving into the White House, and I'm taking an aquarium and a baseball bat" and so on. Each child must remember what has been listed previously as well as add an item of his or her own choice that begins with the next letter of the alphabet. You may allow the students to be either serious or silly in their answers.

• Save newspaper articles that mention the White House to bring to school to share with your students. Talk about the functions that take place there. Note the special guests that are invited to visit the White House.

• Find a jigsaw puzzle that features the White House. Set it up on a table and let your students work on it during November. Talk about its features and its history.

• Send letters from your students to the White House. See the form on page 205. Use one of these addresses:
The President
The White House
1600 Pennsylvania Avenue, NW
Washington, D.C. 20500
e-mail: www.whitehouse.gov

A Tour of the White House Grounds

Be sure each student has a copy of page 201, a pencil and crayons in these colors: blue, red, green, yellow. Look over the diagram briefly with the students before reading these instructions.

1. First write your name in the bottom right corner of your paper.

2. Now look at this picture which shows the White House building and grounds. Did you know that the grounds cover more than 18 acres? Write 18 just above the picture, in the center of the page.

3. The President's office is not in the main building of the White House. It is in a part of the Executive Wing called the Oval Office. Find this on your diagram. Put a blue plus sign on the Oval Office.

4. A more common name for the Executive Wing is the "West Wing." Put a green W on the roof of the West Wing.

5. The Rose Garden is where many parties, receptions and signings take place. Draw a red circle on the Rose Garden.

6. The largest room in the White House is the East Room. It is on the first floor of the main building. It is where state receptions, balls, plays and musicals are held. On the back of your paper, draw a very large rectangle to represent the East Room. Write the words *East Room* in this rectangle. Then turn your paper back over to the front.

7. Did you know that some of the rooms in the main building of the White House have names that are color words? On the first floor you will find the Blue Room, the Red Room and the Green Room. Find the main building. Draw a blue line, a red line and a green line on the top of the main building of the White House.

8. There are five rooms open to the public on the main floor: the Red Room, Blue Room, Green Room, East Room and the State Dining Room. Each of these are used for specific events and are open to the public, usually from 10 a.m. to noon on Tuesdays through Saturday each week. Draw hands on the face of the clock at the bottom of the page to show 10 o'clock.

9. The President and his family live on the second floor of the main building. These rooms are not open to the public. Circle the entire main building with your yellow crayon.

10. Did you know that about one million people visit the White House every year? Which part of the White House would you most like to visit? Put a yellow star on it.

A Tour of the White House Grounds

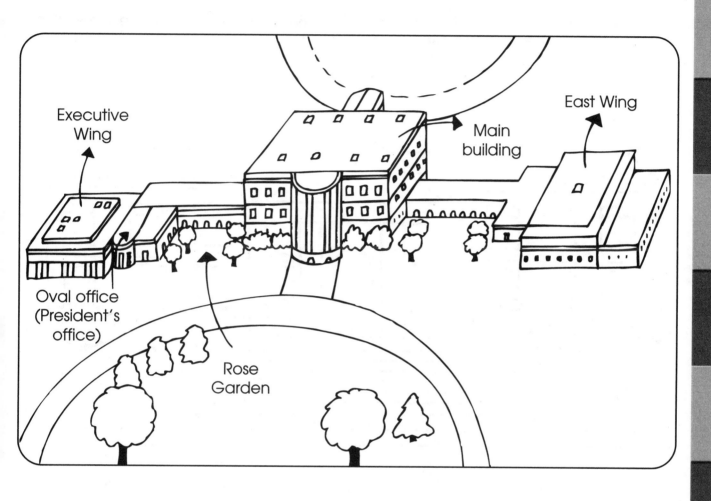

Executive Wing

Main building

East Wing

Oval office (President's office)

Rose Garden

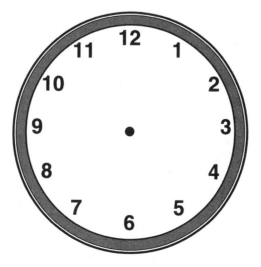

Name _____

A Look at the White House

These two pictures of the White House look alike. But look again. There are some differences! Circle nine things that are different in the bottom picture from the top picture.

Name _____

Read All About It!

Read this article. Then answer the questions below.

In 1792 a special contest was held. What should the new home for the President look like? The person that had the best plan would be the winner. That winner was finally chosen. His name was James Hoban. He worked as an architect and had been born in Ireland. His prize was $500.

Later, there was a war between the U.S. and Britain. In 1814, the British burned the White House. Who do you think was asked to redesign it? That's right. It was James Hoban.

1. What is the best title for this story?
   a. James Hoban, White House Designer
   b. Five Hundred Dollars
   c. The President

2. What does the word *architect* mean?
   a. a President
   b. a person who designs buildings
   c. a person who designs clothes

3. How many times did Mr. Hoban design the White House?
   a. 1
   b. 2
   c. 3

4. What do you think gave Mr. Hoban the idea for the White House?
   a. something on television
   b. a cabin he saw in the woods
   c. a palace in Ireland

5. In what year do you think the work on building the White House began?
   a. 1742
   b. 1792
   c. 1852

6. Why did Mr. Hoban have to redesign the White House?
   a. it was not built well
   b. it was burned
   c. the President did not like it

7. Do you think $500 was a good prize? _____

   Why or why not? _____

   _____

Writing sentences in stories
Write It Right

Here is a story that Polly the parrot wrote about the White House. She did not write the sentences correctly. Cross out each letter that should be a capital letter. Write a capital letter above it. Put a period or a question mark at the end of each sentence.

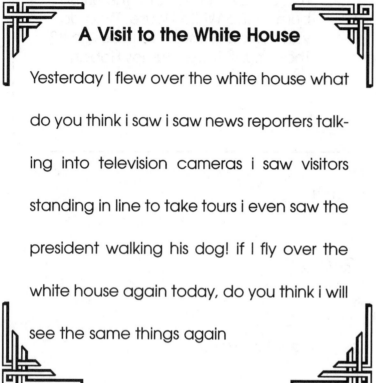

A Visit to the White House

Yesterday I flew over the white house what

do you think i saw i saw news reporters talk-

ing into television cameras i saw visitors

standing in line to take tours i even saw the

president walking his dog! if I fly over the

white house again today, do you think i will

see the same things again

Remember:
- A sentence tells a whole idea.
- Begin the first word of a sentence with a capital letter.
- End a sentence that tells something with a period. (.)
- End a sentence that asks a question with a question mark. (?)

Now write a story as if your were an animal living inside the White House.
Use correct sentences to tell your story.

_____

_____

_____

_____

Name _____

Writing a letter
Dear Mr. President

First think about what you would like to say in a letter to the President of the United States. You may like to encourage him, to thank him for something he's done or to express a view you have on a national topic. Here is a form you may use when writing a letter. Use this as a practice page. If you decide to actually send your letter, rewrite it on a clean sheet of paper. Your teacher will have the address you need.

Heading: Put your address here.

Today's date:

Greeting: For this letter, you should use *Dear Mr. President.*

(Body of the letter goes here. Write your message now.)

Closing: Use a word like *Sincerely,* or *Yours truly,* then sign your name.

Name _____

Less than, greater than

More or Less

Here are some things you might see at the White House. Put < if the first set is less than the second set. Put > if the first set is greater than the second set.

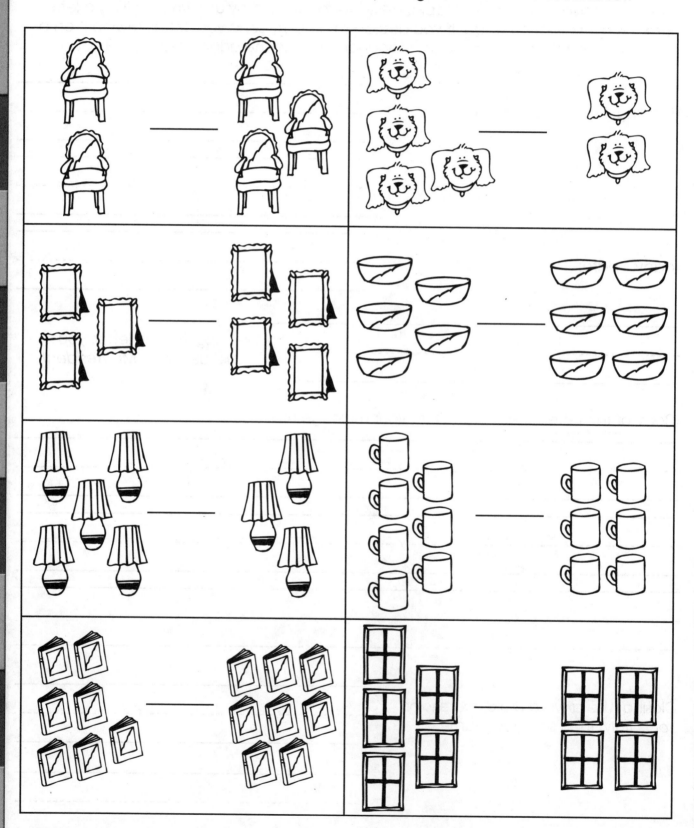

Name _____

Addition
Count the Rooms

Do you know how many rooms there are in the White House? This activity will tell you.
Add the numbers along the trail. Write your answers as you go.
The last number will tell you the number of White House rooms.

TLC10383 Copyright © Teaching & Learning Company, Carthage, IL 62321-0010

Name _____

White House History

Here are some of the interesting events in the history of the White House.
Number them from 1 to 12 to show what happened first, second and so on.

_____ President John Adams and his wife, Abigail, moved into the mansion in 1800.

_____ In 1961 First Lady Jacqueline Kennedy redecorated some of the rooms in the White House, including the Green Room and the Red Room.

_____ From 1815 to 1817, the home was rebuilt.

_____ Gas lighting was added in 1848.

_____ The first stone was put in place in 1792.

_____ In 1891, electricity was installed.

_____ In 1901, it became officially named the White House. (Before that it had been called the President's Palace, the President's House and the Executive Mansion.)

_____ The first water pipes were installed in 1833.

_____ During 1933, a swimming pool was built in the west terrace.

_____ In 1814, the British set fire to the building.

_____ From 1948 to 1952 the building was strengthened and enlarged from 62 to 132 rooms.

_____ An elevator was put in during 1881.

Sandwich Day

November 3 is the day to honor sandwiches. We can all thank the Earl of Sandwich for inventing this popular menu item. The Earl was born on November 3, 1718. He was a lively fellow who enjoyed lots of card games (and gambling). He did not like to take time out to eat with a fork and knife, so he ordered his meat served between two slices of bread. This way he could eat *and* play cards. Sandwiches have become popular with most people today, even those of us who don't want to play cards while we eat!

In this section, you will find a shape book pattern (page 210), a cut-and-paste puzzle (page 211), a poem for choral reading (page 212) and a variety of other skill-based reproducibles.

And no section on sandwiches could be complete without recipes! While many adults enjoy such delights as sardines, corned beef and horseradish, to a child there's nothing quite like the good ol' peanut butter and jelly sandwich. Here are a few variations on this tradition for you and your students to try.

Note: All can be made with either white or wheat bread. All directions are for one sandwich.

Grilled PB and J

Spread one slice of bread with peanut butter and the other slice of bread with your favorite jam or jelly. Put the slices together. Lightly butter the outside of both slices. Brown both sides lightly in an electric skillet.
CAUTION! Only adults should operate the skillet.

Yummy-in-My-Tummy PB and Banana Sandwiches

Start with half of a ripe banana. Break it in chunks into a small bowl. Mash it with a fork. Spread this on one slice of bread. Spread the other slice of bread with peanut butter. Place the two slices together.

PB Deluxe

Spread both slices of bread with peanut butter. On one slice add cooked, crumbled bacon and thin slices of fresh, raw apple. Place the two slices together.

PB and Jelly Butterfly Sandwiches

Make sandwich with peanut butter and jelly. Cut the sandwich into triangles. Arrange on a plate as shown:

Use a carrot or dill pickle spear for a body. Use pieces of a Fruit Roll-Up™ for antennae, if desired.

Shape Book Pattern

Ask students to cut out the two pieces on this page on brown paper to represent bread slices. Next they should cut out several more pages on white, pink, green and/or red paper to represent sandwich fillers such as mayonnaise, ham, lettuce and tomatoes. Pages should then be stapled together. Finally students should write their own sandwich stories, recipes or jokes on the pages in the book.

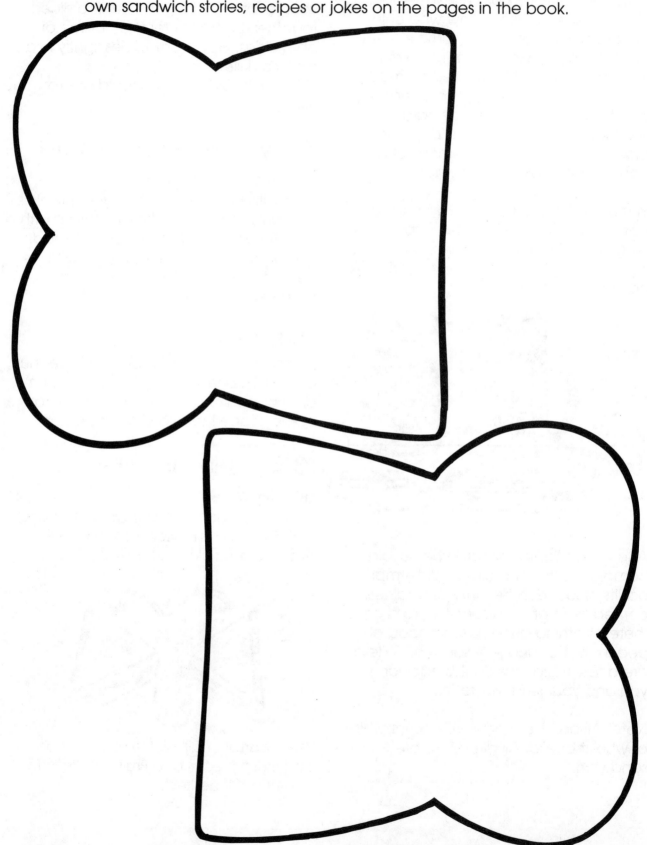

Name _____

Cut-and-paste puzzle
Hot Dog!

Cut out the puzzle pieces. Find out how to put them together to make a hot dog and to spell its name. Then glue the pieces onto a piece of construction paper. Color your hot dog and add your favorite toppings!

Name _____

Teacher: First practice reading this poem aloud altogether several times. Then divide your students into three groups. Have each group take turns reading portions of the poem aloud, as indicated. Switch groups so that students have opportunities to read the other parts, too.

Poem for choral reading

What Goes into a Sandwich?

Group A: What goes into a sandwich?
Can someone tell me, please?

Group B: What goes into a sandwich
Besides bologna and cheese?

Group C: I grow tired of chicken and turkey and ham,
And the same old peanut butter and jam.

Group A: What goes into a sandwich?
Can someone tell me, please?

Group B: There must be something new to try . . .
How about macaroni and cheese?

Group C: Could we use oatmeal or carrots or even red beets?
Or noodles, or rice or our favorite sweets?

Group A: What goes into a sandwich?
Can *you* please tell me soon?

All: If I can't think of something new to try,
I think I'll go live on the moon!

Name _____

Sandwich Cut-Outs

Color the pictures on the next page.
Then cut out the slips of paper on the dotted lines. Put them under the right topic.
When you think you have them all sorted correctly, glue them into place.

Breads	Meats

Spreads	Vegetables

TLC10383 Copyright © Teaching & Learning Company, Carthage, IL 62321-0010

Sandwich Cut-Outs

Use this page with page 213.

ham	peanut butter	lettuce
onion	roast beef	hamburger bun
butter	cucumber	jelly
chicken	mustard	rye
wheat	margarine	barbecued pork
tomato	turkey 	horseradish
ketchup	green pepper	pumper-nickel 
honey	cabbage	bologna

Name _____

ABC Ingredients

What do you like to put in your sandwich? Here are some ideas.
Can you write these words in ABC order? First number the words from 1 to 12.
Then write the words in the correct places.

lettuce	pickles	tomato	eggs
cheese	beef	onion	mustard
ham	nuts	fish	jam

Which two are rhyming words? _____ _____

1. _____ 7. _____

2. _____ 8. _____

3. _____ 9. _____

4. _____ 10. _____

5. _____ 11. _____

6. _____ 12. _____

Logic
Plate Match

Here are lunch plates for four friends, Tasha, Kelsie, Pete and Kyle. Read the clues to find out which plate belongs to each person. Write the correct name under each plate.

Clues
A. Kyle is having fruit with his lunch.
B. Kelsie does not like lettuce.
C. Pete's sandwich is not cut in half.
D. There is lettuce on Tasha's plate.

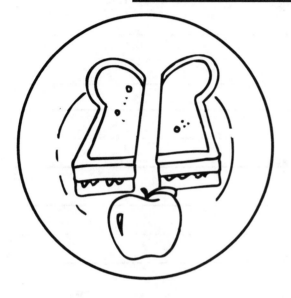

1. _____

2. _____

3. _____

4. _____

TLC10383 Copyright © Teaching & Learning Company, Carthage, IL 62321-0010

Subtraction
Sandwich Riddle

What kind of sandwich can you take underwater? To find out, solve the subtraction problems below. Then find the letter that matches each number. Write the letter in the blank directly under your number. You will spell the answer to the riddle.

A = 1	B = 2	C = 3	D = 4	E = 5
H = 6	I = 7	M = 8	N = 9	R = 10
S = 11	U = 12	W = 13		

$$\begin{array}{r} 9 \\ -\ 8 \\ \hline \end{array} \qquad \begin{array}{r} 44 \\ -\ 33 \\ \hline \end{array} \qquad \begin{array}{r} 20 \\ -\ 8 \\ \hline \end{array} \qquad \begin{array}{r} 11 \\ -\ 9 \\ \hline \end{array} \qquad \begin{array}{r} 13 \\ -\ 5 \\ \hline \end{array} \qquad \begin{array}{r} 15 \\ -\ 14 \\ \hline \end{array}$$

_____   _____   _____   _____   _____   _____

$$\begin{array}{r} 23 \\ -\ 13 \\ \hline \end{array} \qquad \begin{array}{r} 16 \\ -\ 9 \\ \hline \end{array} \qquad \begin{array}{r} 12 \\ -\ 3 \\ \hline \end{array} \qquad \begin{array}{r} 14 \\ -\ 9 \\ \hline \end{array} \qquad \begin{array}{r} 35 \\ -\ 24 \\ \hline \end{array} \qquad \begin{array}{r} 30 \\ -\ 29 \\ \hline \end{array}$$

_____   _____   _____   _____   _____   _____

$$\begin{array}{r} 17 \\ -\ 8 \\ \hline \end{array} \qquad \begin{array}{r} 10 \\ -\ 6 \\ \hline \end{array} \qquad \begin{array}{r} 24 \\ -\ 11 \\ \hline \end{array} \qquad \begin{array}{r} 11 \\ -\ 4 \\ \hline \end{array} \qquad \begin{array}{r} 17 \\ -\ 14 \\ \hline \end{array} \qquad \begin{array}{r} 13 \\ -\ 7 \\ \hline \end{array}$$

_____   _____   _____   _____   _____   _____

What kind of sandwich can you take underwater?

____ _____   _____ !

Reading a bar graph
Mayo's Monsters

Mr. Mayo owns a lot of monsters, and they like some pretty weird sandwiches! He asked each of them to name their favorite kind of sandwich. The results are shown on this graph. Look at the graph, and then answer the questions below.

Mayo's Monsters' Top Sandwiches

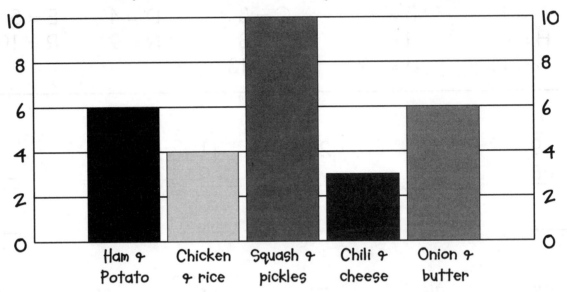

1. What sandwich was chosen the most? _____

2. What sandwich was chosen the least? _____

3. What sandwich was chosen by 4 monsters? _____

4. How many more monsters chose ham and potato than chili and cheese? _____

5. The same number of monsters chose what two kinds of sandwiches?

_____

6. How many monsters in all chose the top 3 sandwiches? _____

7. How many monsters in all chose one of these 5 sandwiches? _____

8. Which one of these sandwiches would *you* like to try? _____

World Kindness Week

World Kindness Week is a recent addition to the list of special days in November. It is sponsored by the Random Acts of Kindness Foundation which was formed in 1995. Its goal is to encourage people to "discover for themselves the power of kindness to effect positive change." To learn more about this foundation, write to them at:

The Random Acts of Kindness Foundation
1801 Broadway Street, Suite 250
Denver, CO 80202

Their web site is a great resource. There you will find free resources including printable lesson plans. The address is: www.actsofkindness.org.

Encourage kindness in your classroom with some of these activities:

- Ask each student to begin a "Kindness Journal." In it, he can write one or two sentences each day about a kind thing he has done. Allow students time to share from their journals during the week.

- Each morning during Kindness Week hold a Kindness Drawing. Put each child's name on a slip of paper. Put the papers into a bag. Instruct each child to draw out another child's name and to keep it a secret. (If someone draws her own name, she will need to put it back and draw another.) Students should try to do at least one kind thing for the child whose name she drew. At the end of the day, ask each student to guess who drew his name. Return the slips to the bag so they can be redrawn the next day. Consider extending this activity throughout the year. For instance, every Tuesday could be Kindness Day, and the drawing could be held on that day each week for the rest of the school year.

- Send "Kind Word Certificates." Use the forms on page 220. The top certificate is to be used by students who want to write a kind written message to give to another student or to take home for a family member. The bottom certificates are for you to award to those students that you "catch" being kind.

- Participate in a service project. Two suggestions:
Visit a nearby seniors' center, nursing home or hospital. Chat with patients or deliver homemade cards and sing a song.
Ask your school maintenance staff if there are simple cleaning tasks your students can help perform. Or perhaps your school office staff could use help stapling, collating or delivering newsletters to classrooms.

- Check out the great books listed on page 226. Several of the books tell stories of the "ripple effect" of showing kindness to others. You will also find a song on page 221 and reproducible skill pages on pages 222-225.

Kind Word Certificates

This "Kind Words" certificate is awarded to

_____

The kind words I would like to share with you today are

_____

_____

_____

Have a great day!

From _____ Date _____

I caught YOU being kind!

Name _____

I'm so proud of you!

Signed _____

Date _____

I heard your very kind words!

Date _____

spoken by

_____

Keep up the good work!

Signed _____

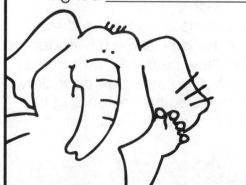

Name _____

Fill the World with Kindness

To the tune of "London Bridge"

This is what I'll do today,
Do today, do today.
This is what I'll do today
To fill the world with kindness.

I'll find a friend and share with her,
Share with her, share with her.
I'll find a friend and share with her,
To fill the world with kindness.

I'll phone someone who's all alone,
All alone, all alone.
I'll phone someone who's all alone,
To fill the world with kindness.

I'll find a child and play with him,
Play with him, play with him.
I'll find a child and play with him,
To fill the world with kindness.

I'll find some trash and pick it up,
Pick it up, pick it up.
I'll find some trash and pick it up,
To fill the world with kindness.

Allow students to make up more stanzas of their own.
They may also want to add actions.

Days of the week
Daily Kindness

Here are seven kind things you could do at home. Write in the name of one of the days of week for each one, to show what you might try to do each day. You can write the names in any order you choose.

| Sunday |
| Monday |
| Tuesday |
| Wednesday |
| Thursday |
| Friday |
| Saturday |

1. On _____ I can set the table.

2. On _____ I can empty the trash can.

3. On _____ I can phone a friend or relative.

4. On _____ I can care for a pet.

5. On _____ I can make a picture for someone.

6. On _____ I can pick up my room.

7. On _____ I can help _____ with

_____ .

Make a picture on the back for one of these sentences.

Name _____

Antonyms
Vine Time

During World Kindness Week, you will probably try extra hard to be nice to people around you. Of course, that is something you should try to do *all* the time. The opposite of being kind is being mean. You know many other opposites, too, like *hot and cold,* and *happy and sad.* Look at each word in the box. Find the word on the vine that means the opposite. Write the word on the vine next to its opposite. One is done for you.

day	up	tall	new
quiet	above	big	fast

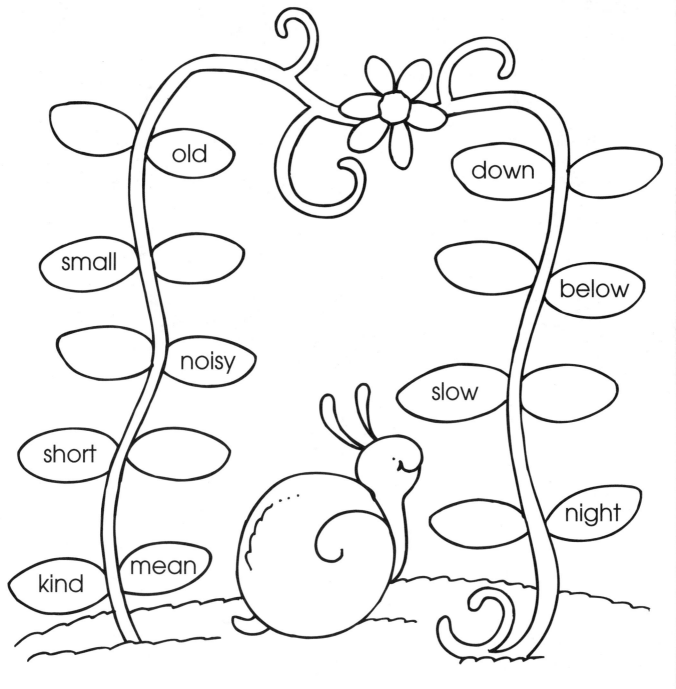

old

down

small

below

noisy

slow

short

night

kind   mean

Subjects and predicates

Kind Subjects

Every sentence has two parts.
The subject, or naming part, tells who or what the sentence is about.
The predicate, or telling part, tells what the subject does or did.
Draw a line from each subject to the right predicate.
You will learn about some things others did for World Kindness Week.

Subjects	Predicates
The librarian	took our dog for a walk.
Gary	shared her birthday cake.
A silly clown	helped us find books.
My brother and I	raked his neighbor's leaves.
Mom	made us laugh.

Now read each sentence. Circle the subject. Underline the predicate.

Jen helped her sister fly a kite.

My grandparents took me out for ice cream.

Mrs. Jackson showed us a good video.

Our family cleaned out the garage.

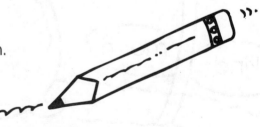

Name _____

Adding coin values

Casey's Coins

Casey has dumped all the coins out of his piggy bank.
He wants to find something special to buy for his little sister.
Help him figure out how many coins are needed for each toy.
Read the price of each item. Circle that amount of money.

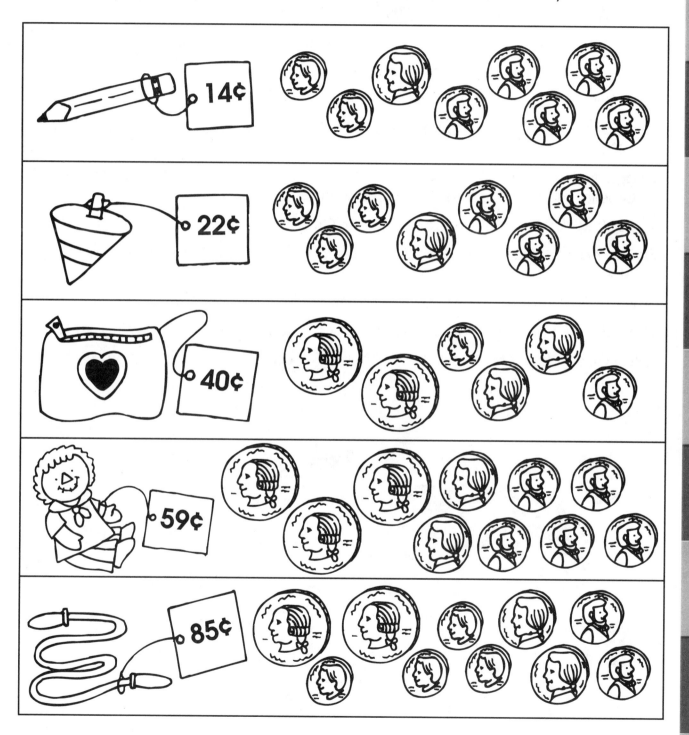

Color the items. Circle the one you think Casey should buy for his sister.

Resources

Because Brian Hugged His Mother by David L. Rice. Dawn Publications, 1999.

Celia and the Sweet, Sweet Water by Katherine Paterson. Houghton Mifflin, 1998.

The Child's World of Kindness by Jan Belk Moncure. The Child's World, Inc., 1996.

The Chicken Soup for Little Souls: The Goodness Gorillas by Mark V. Hansen. Health Communications, Inc., 1997.

Glenna's Seeds by Nancy Edwards. Child Welfare League of American, Inc., 2000.

Hunter and His Dog by Brian Wildsmith. Oxford University Press, 2000.

I Like Your Buttons by Sarah Marwil Lamstein. Albert Whitman, 1999.

Perfect Porridge: A Story About Kindness by Rochel Sandman. Hachai Publishing, 2000.

Raggedy Ann's Candy Heart Wisdom: Words of Love and Friendship by Johnny Gruelle. Simon & Schuster Children's Division, 1998.

The Sidewalk Patrol by Larry Dane Brimner. Grolier, 2002.

Simple Acts of Kindness for Kids: Little Ways to Make a Big Difference by Ray Alonzo. Trade Life Books, 1999.

Small Acts of Kindness by James Vollbracht. Paulist Press, 1997.

Thread of Kindness: A Tzedakah Story by Leah P. Shollar. Hachai Publishing, 2000.

Three Good Blankets by Ida Luttrell. Simon & Schuster's Children's Division, 1991.

National Children's Book Week

National Children's Book Week comes each November, usually the week before Thanksgiving. What a great time to encourage your students to try out some new books! The next several pages are packed with ideas to help your class celebrate this special week.

Here is a bulletin board idea to get you started:

Ask each student to complete a fish for a book he reads during Book Week. He can trace the fish patterns from page 228 onto colored paper, and then cut it out. On the front of the fish he should write the author and title of the book. On the back, he should write his name. Cut out a partial "boat" from newsprint or a brown paper sack. The fishing rod could be a long stick or strip of black paper. Make the fish line from dental floss and the hook from poster board wrapped in aluminum foil. Happy Fishing!

Name _____

Memory game
Classic Matchup

Here's a memory game for two students to play together. In this game, students will match titles of classic children's books with their authors. First copy this page onto heavy paper. Cut out the playing cards and laminate all of them, including the key. (You may choose to let students check their own answers.) To play, all cards should be placed facedown on a table. Player one turns over two cards. If he makes a match, he keeps the cards. If the cards do not match, he turns them over and leaves them in their original spots. Then player two takes a turn. Play continues until all the cards have been matched. The winner is the child with the most cards.

You may want to expand this set of cards to include additional titles and authors. Students may also want to make a pair of cards for a book that they read this week.

Curious George 	H.A. Rey	Horton Hears a Who	Dr. Seuss
Where the Wild Things Are	Maurice Sendak	Madeline 	Ludwig Bemelmans
Where the Sidewalk Ends 	Shel Silverstein	Winnie the Pooh 	A.A. Milne

Name _____

Finding the main idea
Cover Story

Read the sentence that tells about each story.
Then circle the book cover that best shows the main idea of that story.

1. This story tells how Ed visits farms to care for sick animals.

A.    B.

2. This story tells how we usually celebrate Thanksgiving.

A.    B.

3. This book contains poems about weather, plants and animals.

A.    B.    C.

4. This story is told by a boy who loves his grandfather.

A.    B.    C.

5. This book explains how to learn the names of trees by studying their leaves.

A.    B.    C.

230

Name _____

Reading Circle

Here's a book report form you've probably never seen before.
It goes around in a circle! The next time you finish reading a book, try to complete it.
Start at the arrow, and fill in each space that you find. Don't get dizzy.

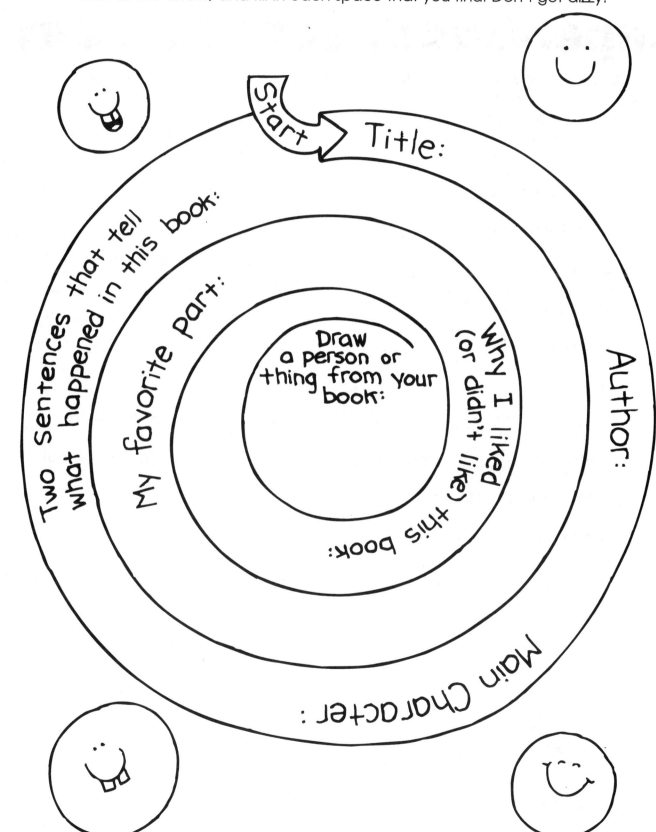

Start

Title:

Author:

Two Sentences that tell what happened in this book:

My favorite part:

Draw a person or thing from your book:

Why I liked (or didn't like) this book:

Main Character:

Name _____

*Teachers: Read the book, **Alexander and the Terrible, Horrible, No Good, Very Bad Day** by Judith Viorst**
with your class before introducing this activity.

Pattern writing

The Wonderful, Fabulous, Super-Good, Very Fine Day

You know all about Alexander's terrible day. Now let's think about the very opposite sort of day in which everything goes very well. Imagine what a wonderful day for *you* might be like. Fill in the blanks to write your own story. (This is slightly shorter than the real book.) Then make a small book from construction paper. Copy your story into the book and add illustrations.

I went to bed with _____, and

when I woke up this morning there was _____

and when I got out of bed this morning I _____

and by mistake in the sink I found _____

and I could tell it was going to be a wonderful, fabulous, super-good, very fine

day.

At breakfast _____ found a _____ in his/her cereal

box and _____ found a _____ in his/her cereal box, but

in *my* cereal box I found _____. I don't

want to move anywhere!

At school, the teacher liked my _____ better than

_____. At singing time she said _____

_____. At counting time she said _____

_____. Aren't I swell? I could tell it was going to be a

wonderful, fabulous, super-good, very fine day.

*Second Aladdin Paperbacks edition, 1987. Also available in other editions.

After school my mom took us all to the dentist and _____

_____. On the way downstairs,

_____ and while we were waiting for my mom

to go get the car _____. I am

having a wonderful, fabulous, super-good, very fine day, I told everybody, and

everyone heard me. I don't want to move anywhere!

Then we went to the _____ store to buy _____.

I chose _____ and the man said _____.

When we picked up my dad at the office he said I could play with the

_____ , and this is what happened: _____

_____. My dad said _____

_____. I am having a wonderful, fabulous, super-good,

very fine day!

There were _____ for supper and I *LOVE* _____.

There was _____ on TV and I *LOVE* _____.

My bath was just right, I got to play with _____, I found my lost

_____ and I got to wear my _____ pajamas.

I *LOVE* my _____ pajamas! When I went to bed _____

_____.

It has been a wonderful, fabulous, super-good, very fine day! My mom says

some days are like that, and she doesn't want me to move anywhere.

Multiplication with cents
Overdue

Forgetful Floyd likes to read books to learn how to do all sorts of things.
But he has a terrible time remembering to return his library books.
Poor Floyd has eight overdue books, and he checked each one out on a different day.
Now that it's National Children's Book Week, he is finally returning the books.
The fine for an overdue book at the Sometown Library is 2¢ for every day the book is late.
Find out what the fine is for each book. Write the correct number in the blank.

1. How to Make Mud Pies by I. like Dirt	3 days late Fine: _____ ¢		2. How to Make Cream Pies by I. like Milk	5 days late Fine: _____ ¢
3. You Can Build a Clubhouse by Iva Hammer	8 days late Fine: _____ ¢		4. Good Rules for Clubhouse Gangs by Bea Kind	9 days late Fine: _____ ¢
5. All About Motorcycles by David Harley	12 days late Fine: _____ ¢		6. Save Gas: Ride a Bike by P. Edal	6 days late Fine: _____ ¢
7. How to Read Music by Dee Sharp	10 days late Fine: _____ ¢		8. You Can Play the Piano by B. Lack Keys	20 days late Fine: _____ ¢

Make up a silly book title and author of your own. Then draw a book cover for it.

Thanksgiving

Thanksgiving is a favorite holiday of many Americans, and perhaps *your* students. It's a time for family, food and, yes, for giving thanks for all we enjoy. This section includes some ideas for celebrating this special time with your students. Notice the interactive bulletin board on pages 236-237. You will also find a variety of skill reproducibles on pages 239-244.

Additional suggestions include:

- Talk about the *cornucopia*. Explain that its other name is *horn of plenty*. It is a very old symbol that's used to represent a bountiful harvest. It is usually filled with fall fruits and vegetables. If possible, bring a wicker cornucopia into the classroom and ask students to bring apples, grapes, squash, gourds, etc., to fill it. Place all these items together with the cornucopia on a display table.

- Make books called *The ABCs of Thanksgiving*. Challenge your students to think of one thing for which they are thankful for each letter of the alphabet. Use the cornucopia shape book patterns on page 238. Students should use the shape to trace plain white paper pages. Arrange the pages so that students can write on both the front and the back. Tell students they may either write the word, draw the object or both for each letter of the alphabet. Cut colored paper for book covers. Decorate the covers with the title given here, and/or student's choice of fall artwork. (Hint: Here are some ideas for tricky letters: j—Jell-O™, jam, jets; k—kites, kazoos, a friend named Kate; q—quarters, quiche, quilts, quiz games; z—zipper, zinnias, zero, zoo.)

- Plan a Thanksgiving party before your students go on their holiday break. Game: Play a Thanksgiving version of "I'm Thinking Of..." Choose one child to go first. He thinks of an item for which he is thankful and gives clues to the rest of the class. The first one to guess the item correctly chooses the next object. For example, Tara might decide she is thankful for her family's car. She might give these hints: "I'm thankful for something that moves a lot. It is large and blue. I can sit in it," and so on. Food: See page 187 for several ideas related to corn which came from Native Americans. Also, consider making turkey cupcakes. Use a regular cake mix (or muffin mix) and follow package directions to make cupcakes or muffins. Decorate with vanilla or chocolate frosting and multicolored sprinkles. Cut out one of the turkey patterns for each student. Ask students to color them. Then attach two toothpicks to the turkey and insert the picks into the side of the cupcake as shown. Serve apple cider or juice for a beverage. Decorations: In addition to the classroom cornucopia described on the left, be on the lookout for "Indian corn" to place in the classroom. You can also ask students to hang brown, orange and yellow streamers around the classroom.

Thanksgiving

Ask students to spell words using only the letters in *Thanksgiving*. Each student should write his word on a feather and then attach it to the correct turkey. Words that start with letters other than s, t, g and h can be traced onto leaves and put around the edges to form a border. Words should contain three or more letters. Ask students to predict which turkey will have the most feathers by Thanksgiving. Sample words:

S—sag, sank, sat, shin, sing, sink, sit, skit, stag

H—hag, hang, has, hat, hint, hit

T—tag, tan, tank, task, think, tin

G—gain, gas, giant, gnat

Others—ant, ask, kin, king, nag, van

Shape Book Pattern

Name _____

Gobble, Gobble!

Can you find the two turkeys that are *exactly* alike?
Circle the pair of matching turkeys. Then color all of them.

A.

B.

C.

D.

E.

F.

Identifying missing consonants
Thanksgiving Feast

Everyone loves to eat a great big meal on Thanksgiving Day.
Many of the foods we like are spelled with double consonants. Read the clues to find out what letters are missing in each word below. Write in the missing double letters.

1. Mom puts stu_ _ ing inside the turkey. Sometimes it is also called

    dre _ _ ing.

2. Grandpa likes to eat cranbe_ _ y sauce with his turkey.

3. Dad's favorite fall food is our homemade a_ _lesauce.

4. Tom offers to scrape ca_ _ots, so we can cook them with butter and

    honey.

5. Have you ever tasted my grandmother's corn mu_ _ ins or whole-

    wheat ro_ _ s?

6. I like pumpkin pie best, but Bobbie prefers che_ _y pie for her

    de_ _ ert.

7. Don't forget to spell the sound that a turkey makes, "Go_ _le,

    go_ _ le!"

On the back of this page, draw a picture of your favorite Thanksgiving foods.

Listening comprehension

The First Thanksgiving

The first Thanksgiving was held in 1621. It was a celebration held by Pilgrims who began the Plymouth Colony. This area is now part of Massachusetts. The Pilgrims invited their new Native American friends to their celebration. These friends had taught the Pilgrims how to grow food in their new land. The Native Americans were part of the Wampanoag (*wampa NO og*) tribe. They brought gifts of food to the first Thanksgiving. The Pilgrims gave thanks to God for their crops, their food and their new friends.

Two years later there was a drought, or a long period with no rain. The Pilgrims had a day of fasting and prayer. While they were praying, the rains began! Then the day was changed to one of Thanksgiving. Slowly it became a yearly custom to hold a day of Thanksgiving each year after the harvest.

Now the American Thanksgiving is held on the fourth Thursday in November every year. In Canada, Thanksgiving is held on the second Monday in October. All of us still have a lot for which to be thankful today.

1. During what year did the first Thanksgiving take place? *(1621)*

2. Where did the Pilgrims live who held the first Thanksgiving celebration? *(Plymouth Colony, or Massachusetts)*

3. What did the Native Americans bring? *(food)*

4. From what tribe were they? *(Wampanoag)*

5. What is a drought? *(a long period with no rain)*

6. Two years after the first Thanksgiving, what happened when the Pilgrims were fasting and praying for rain? *(It started to rain.)*

7. Do you know what it means "to fast"? *(It means to intentionally go without eating.)*

8. After what event did Americans begin to celebrate Thanksgiving every year? *(the harvest)*

9. When do Americans have Thanksgiving? *(on the fourth Thursday in November)*

10. When do Canadians have Thanksgiving? *(on the second Monday in October)*

Name _____

Writing subjects and predicates
Kitchen Caper

This picture shows Rosa's family preparing for Thanksgiving. See how busy they are! Look at the sentences below the picture. Write a subject or predicate to finish each sentence so that the sentence tells about the picture.

1. Rosa _____.

2. _____ is peeling potatoes.

3. Rosa's brother, Peter, _____.

4. _____ is stuffing the turkey.

5. Socks, the cat, _____.

6. _____ is a special day that comes just once a year.

7. The whole family _____.

242

TLC10383 Copyright © Teaching & Learning Company, Carthage, IL 62321-0010

Name _____

Counting by fives
Turkey Trail

Travis Turkey likes Farmer Jones and his family, but he really doesn't want to become their Thanksgiving dinner. Travis is looking for a way to escape from the barnyard into the woods, just for a few days until the holiday is over. Can you help him find the way? Start at the 5 by Travis. Then draw a line to the 10. Continue to draw a line from number to number as you count by fives until Travis is safely into the woods.

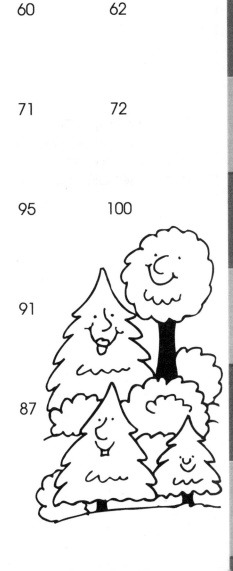

5	10	12	47	50	54
23	15	16	45	58	55
20	24	41	40	60	62
25	29	35	65	71	72
26	30	70	90	95	100
32	75	34	85	91	
76	79	80	83	87	

Word problems
Holiday Numbers
Solve each Thanksgiving word problem.
Use the space in each box to do your work. Write your answer in the little box.

---

1. Mom is baking 2 pumpkin pies. Uncle Joe is making 3 apple pies. Cousin Suzy is making 2 cherry pies. How many pies are there altogether?

2. Mary's recipe for cranberry salad calls for 10 ounces of fresh cranberries. Mary wants to make 3 of these salads. How many ounces of cranberries will she need?

---

3. Everyone will eat 2 slices of turkey. There are 12 people. How many slices of turkey do we need?

4. It takes Dad 5 minutes to peel 2 potatoes. How long will it take him to peel 4 potatoes?

---

5. Cindy baked 7 pies for her family's huge Thanksgiving dinner. She gave 2 of those pies to her neighbor. How many pies did she have left?

6. Sam likes apple pie the best. He has 3 pies, and he wants to cut each one into 8 pieces. How many pieces of pie will he have?

---

7. Grandma bought 20 pounds of potatoes. She used 3 pounds to make potato salad. She used 4 pounds for baked potatoes. How many pounds does she have left for mashed potatoes?

8. Heidi has candy corn to share with her 8 Thanksgiving guests. If she gives each guest 9 pieces of candy corn, how many pieces will she give away in all?

Bookmarks, Name Tag & Certificate

Be Kind — Share a Book

Books Are a Great Catch!

Hi! I'm ___ name

This Nifty November Award is presented to

_____

for a Super Job!

Sign: _____
Date: _____

December

Get ready for a delightful December with a festive assortment of bulletin boards, teacher helps and curriculum reproducible pages to see you through December's holidays and special days.

We've chosen six special themes for this month: bingo's birthday month, the anniversary of basketball, the discovery of the South Pole, Hanukkah, Christmas and Kwanzaa. For some of these themes you will find bulletin boards, recipes, games and resource lists. For *all* of the units you will have appealing reproducibles that cover important primary grade skills. Most skill sheets are for math or language, but we've also included some pages for science, social studies and general thinking skills.

Simply pick the themes and select activities and worksheets that are on an appropriate level for your students. You will be able to use many ideas in each unit even though some individual pages may be too difficult or too easy for your particular class.

First your students will wish a "happy birthday" to the ever-popular game of bingo. In this section you will find game cards and word lists so that students can play bingo while they practice what they've learned about arithmetic, antonyms and more.

Next, your students will be "hoop"ing it up as they celebrate basketball's anniversary. We've included many physical education activities, a bulletin board and reproducible pages covering counting, compound words, comparing and contrasting and more.

Roald Amundsen became the first person to reach the South Pole on December 14, 1911. Celebrate this historic day as your students work with mittens, dogsleds and penguins through a variety of skill pages. Don't miss the countdown action poem and the list of resources for this chilling topic.

Hanukkah comes to life with our traditional and background information. A word search and hidden picture are among the features here.

Christmas crafts and gift ideas include a simple, colorful bulletin board and shape book in addition to an assortment of language and math reproducibles. Initial consonants, ABC order, subjects and predicates, coordinates and coins are some of the skills covered.

A brief section on Kwanzaa completes this monthly collection. Take time to teach (and learn) about this interesting celebration. You'll find some suggested resources listed, along with two skill pages.

Don't forget all the great clip art on the CD. It promises to make for a truly delightful December in *your* classroom!

Happy Birthday, Bingo!

The game of bingo was first manufactured in December 1929, by Edwin S. Lowe. It's now a popular fund-raiser. One estimate states that the game raises five billion dollars a year for charities. But you and your students can have lots of learning fun *without* money! Begin with some simple letter identification as young students practice spelling the word *bingo* with the cut-and-paste activity on page 249. Next, recognize that bingo presents a terrific game format to use in the classroom as you practice many important skills. Look at the game cards on page 250. Duplicate this page so that you have one card for each student. Then use one of these variations for a whole-class game:

Math

Instruct students to write the numbers 1-24 in any arrangement on their cards. Reproduce the math problems on page 251. (Choose the set of problems that is more appropriate for your class.) Cut the problems apart and place the slips of paper into a paper sack. To play the game, draw out one slip of paper and read the math problem aloud. Ask students to figure out the answer and cover that number wherever it appears on their cards. Keep playing until a student has five markers in a row, horizontally, vertically or diagonally. Have the winning student(s) read back their answers so you can check their computations. Note: Every student will be using the same numbers, and every math problem yields one of those numbers. Consequently, every student should be able to cover a number with each draw.

Language

- Reading: Make your own list of sight words, spelling words or vocabulary words to use. Write them on the board, and ask each student to copy any 24 of the words into any box on his card. Randomly call out words from the list. If the child can find the word on his card, he covers it. After reaching a "bingo," each student must correctly read back his words to you.

- Antonyms: Use the master list at the top of page 252. Write these words on the board, and ask each student to copy them in any order onto his card. Reproduce the list at the bottom of the page. Cut these words apart and put them into a sack from which to draw. Call out each word as you draw it. Students should cover the words from their cards that are antonyms, or opposites, of the word you drew. Double-check answers by having winners read their words back to you.

- Synonyms and Homonyms: Make your own word lists and follow the directions above.

- Contractions: Use the master list of contractions at the top of page 253. Write these words on the board, and ask each student to copy them in any order onto his card. Use the word pairs at the bottom of the page to draw from a bag. Call out each word as you draw it. Students should cover the matching contractions on their cards.

Health

Put words from the master list at the top of page 254 on the board. Ask students to choose only the healthy foods from the list to copy into spaces on their bingo cards. Then cut up the foods listed on the bottom half of the page to draw out of a bag.

Don't miss the phonics activity on page 255 and the song ideas on page 256. Have a Happy Birthday, Bingo Month!

Name _____

Spell It!

Cut out the letters and paste them on another piece of paper to spell *bingo*. Watch out!
There are extra letters that you don't need, and some letters are upside down.
Get the right letters going in the right direction on your page.
Spell *bingo* in both uppercase and lowercase letters as shown here: bingo, BINGO.

N	g	m	u
b	p	l	o
p	O	d	G
B	L	i	M

Bingo Cards

		FREE		

		FREE		

Math Bingo

See page 248 for instructions.

Addition and Subtraction

1 + 0	3 - 1	2 + 1	6 - 2
14 - 9	9 - 3	12 - 5	10 -2
4 + 5	11 - 1	4 + 7	6 + 6
6 + 7	7 + 7	20 - 5	19 - 3
9 + 8	9 + 9	20 - 1	10 + 10
25 - 4	11 + 11	25 - 2	12 + 12

Multiplication, Division, Addition and Subtraction

1 x 1	6 ÷ 3	9 ÷ 3	2 x 2
25 ÷ 5	30 ÷ 5	14 ÷ 2	24 ÷ 3
27 ÷ 3	100 ÷ 10	33 ÷ 3	4 x 3
9 + 4	6 + 8	5 x 3	4 x 4
21 - 4	3 x 6	11 + 8	5 x 4
3 x 7	19 + 3	16 + 7	8 x 3

Antonym Bingo

See page 248 for instructions.

Master list to put on the board

first	stop	slow	yes
right	open	asleep	work
many	quiet	happy	short
day	old	kind	hard
up	in	above	hot
empty	push	lost	front

List to copy and cut apart for draws

last	start	fast	no
left	shut	awake	play
few	noisy	sad	tall
night	new	mean	soft
down	out	below	cold
full	pull	found	back

Contraction Bingo

See page 248 for instructions.

Master list to put on the board

aren't	you're	hasn't	they're
haven't	we're	hadn't	it's
I'll	I'm	shouldn't	we've
couldn't	we'll	you've	she's
he's	don't	doesn't	isn't
didn't	won't	wasn't	you've

List to copy and cut apart for draws

are not	you are	has not	they are
have not	we are	had not	it is
I will	I am	should not	we have
could not	we will	you have	she is
he is	do not	does not	is not
did not	will not	was not	you have

Healthy Bingo

See page 248 for instructions.

Master list to put on the board

apple	potato chips	cookies	chicken	lettuce	milk
soda	orange juice	carrots	peaches	dough-nuts	tuna
cake	whole-wheat bread	corn	celery	tomatoes	beans
plum	grape juice	corn flakes	straw-berries	peas	yogurt
pear	cottage cheese	lean beef	potatoes	rice	candy

List to copy and cut apart for draws

apple	cottage cheese	chicken	lettuce
milk	lean beef	potatoes	tuna
plum	orange juice	carrots	peaches
pear	corn	celery	whole-wheat bread
beans	tomatoes	peas	yogurt
rice	grape juice	corn flakes	strawberries

Name _____

Initial consonant sounds

Bingo Sounds

Look at this bingo card. Under each letter there should be only pictures of words that begin with that letter. For example, under the B, there should be only pictures of B words. There is one incorrect picture under each letter. Find that picture and put an X on it. Then color the rest of the pictures.

TLC10383 Copyright © Teaching & Learning Company, Carthage, IL 62321-0010

255

Song
B-I-N-G-O

You probably already know the old favorite song called "B-I-N-G-O."
Do your students know it? Ask them to sing it along with you.
Here are the words, along with a few variations.

There was a farmer who had a dog,
And BINGO was his name-o.
B-I-N-G-O, B-I-N-G-O, B-I-N-G-O
And BINGO was his name-o.

Sing it through a second time, replacing the B with a clap each time the dog's name is spelled.

Sing it through a third time, replacing the B and I with a clap each time the dog's name is spelled and so on.

Variations:
Instead of a clap, replace each letter with a stomp of the foot, a nod of the head or a snap of the fingers.

For a really tricky version, replace the B with a clap, the I with a stomp, the N with a nod, the G with a snap and the O with a silent "O" formed with the mouth.

Make up an entire new song about a new silly or serious five-letter word. Here are two ideas:

There was a duck who made a noise
And Quack was his name-o
Q-U-A-C-K, Q-U-A-C-K, Q-U-A-C-K,
And Quack was his name-o.

There was a woman who stayed up late
And EARLY was her name-o
E-A-R-L-Y, E-A-R-L-Y, E-A-R-L-Y,
And Early was her name-o.

(Can your students think of other opposites to sing about?)

The Anniversary of Basketball

On December 1, 1891, a teacher of physical education at the International YMCA Training School in Springfield, Massachusetts, invented the game of basketball. His name was James Naismith, and he wanted to find a sport that students could play indoors during the winter months. He nailed peach baskets up at opposite ends of the balcony in the gym and gave students soccer balls to toss into them. The game of basketball has come a long way since then! Celebrate the anniversary of this popular sport all during December with some of the activities found in this unit.

You can accentuate any subject area with the bouncy bulletin board idea shown on page 259. Counting, forming sentences and ordering numbers are some of the skills that appear on reproducibles for pages 260-266. And of course, you must incorporate some physical education with this topic!

Most primary grade students will not be able to participate in a game where all the skills and rules of competitive basketball are followed. There are some simple "lead-up" games, however, where your students can practice some basketball skills. Try these with softer playground balls:

- **Hot Potato** (tossing and catching)
  Students should sit in a circle an arm's length apart from each other. On a "go" signal, the ball is tossed around the circle until the "stop" signal is given. The student left holding the ball gets a point. If someone gets three points, he has to sit in the center of the circle for one turn.

- **Teacher Ball** (tossing, bouncing and catching)
  Arrange students in several circles, each containing six to eight children. Give each group one ball. One child (the "teacher") stands in the center of the circle and tosses the ball to each member of the circle. When the teacher has tossed to each person in the circle, she rejoins the circle and a new "teacher" goes into the center. Variation: Instead of tossing the ball, the "teacher" may bounce it to each child.

- **Teacher Ball Relay Race**
  Be sure each circle has exactly the same number of players. Play the game described above as a relay. Each circle competes against the other circles to see which group can pass (or bounce) the ball around the circle first.

- **Call Ball** (vertical tossing and catching)
  Arrange students in circles with one playground ball for each group of eight to 10 students. The leader stands in the center of the circle and tosses the ball into the air while calling another player's name. The player called must run forward and try to catch the ball before it hits the ground (or after one bounce). If he is successful, he becomes the new leader and tosses the ball as he calls another name. Otherwise, the original leader tosses the ball into the air again.

- **Stop and Go** (running, stopping and starting)
Players stand side by side at one end of the playing area. A goal line should be marked 50-60 feet away. The teacher blows a whistle and the students start to run toward the goal line. When the whistle is blown again, the students must run in the opposite direction. The game continues with the blowing (at irregular intervals), stopping and starting until someone reaches the goal line.

- **Flowers and the Wind** (running and dodging)
Divide the class into two groups. The groups should stand about 60 feet apart and face each other. One group is called the "flowers." This group must secretly decide which kind of flower they are. The other group is the wind. The flowers advance toward the wind while the other group tries to guess what kind of flower they are. The wind calls out flower names. When the correct flower name is called, the flowers turn around and run back to their goal while the wind chases them. Anyone tagged by the wind joins that team. Then the teams switch roles and play the game again.

- **Kangaroo Race** (leg strength)
Divide the class into teams of six to eight students each. Establish a starting line and a turning point 20-30 feet away. The first player on each team must get into a semi-crouched position and hop like a kangaroo to the turning point and back. Then the next person on the team does the same. Continue until all the players on one team have done the hop.

- **Frog Hop** (leg strength)
Follow the instructions for the Kangaroo Race described above except that the players must squat down and lay their hands on the starting line. They are to push with their feet, extend their bodies forward and land on their hands.

- **Dribble Relay** (dribbling)
Divide the class into teams of six to eight students each. Give each team a basketball. Set up a starting line and a turning point 20-30 feet away. The first player on each team must dribble the ball to the turning point and back, and then give the ball to the next player on the team. (You may specify if you want students to use their left hand, right hand, either or both.) The winning team is the one in which all players finish dribbling first.

- Don't forget the old favorites such as dodgeball; kickball and Duck, Duck Goose. All of these allow the students to practice running, stopping and starting.

- Also encourage students to try to make baskets into a lowered hoop.

Anniversary of Basketball

Curious George by H.A. Rey

Antarctica by Helen Cowcher

Hoop–Hoop–Hooray for Reading!

Tacky the Penguin by Helen Lester

Where the Wild Things Are by Maurice Sendak

Green Eggs and Ham by Dr. Seuss

Madeline by Ludwig Bemelmans

December 1st is the anniversary of basketball

Use a dark background. Use bright orange for the basketballs. Draw a net using a black marker on white paper, or attach an actual piece of netting from a bag in which oranges or potatoes are sold.

Caption can be changed for almost any subject area:

Hoop-Hoop-Hooray for Reading—Students write the titles and authors of books they're reading on the balls.

Hoop-Hoop-Hooray for Math—Students write math facts on the basketballs.

Hoop-Hoop-Hooray for Animals—Students write the names of mammals on one ball, insects on another ball, reptiles on a third ball and so on.

Hoop-Hoop-Hooray for Our State—Students write important facts about their state on the balls.

Counting, noting details

Basketball Barb

Barb loves the game of basketball. You can tell by looking at her bedroom! How many basketballs can you count in her room? Write the number here. _____
Then color the picture.

Name _____

Basketball Scramble

Can you unscramble these sentences about basketball? Write the words in the correct order on the blank below the words. Remember to begin each sentence with a capital letter and to end each one with a period.

1. net rim hangs a from the basketball

   _____

2. worth a goal is points two field

   _____

3. a throw worth is free point one

   _____

4. court the is rectangle basketball a

   _____

5. filled air ball the with is

   _____

6. players are there five a team on

   _____

7. famous is Michael Jordan player basketball a

   _____

Reading comprehension
Read-Aloud Article

Here is part of an article about Michael Jordan, the great basketball player.
Read the article along with your teacher, and then answer the questions below.

Michael Jordan has sometimes been called the most famous athlete in the world. He is famous for leaping high into the air to make his "slam dunk" baskets. He even earned the nickname of Air Jordan.

Michael Jeffrey Jordan was born in 1963 in Brooklyn, New York. He grew up in Wilmington, North Carolina. He attended the University of North Carolina and played basketball on his university's team.

In 1984 Jordan joined the Chicago Bulls, a professional basketball team. He helped that team win four championships. He was named the most valuable player in each championship series.

In 1984 and 1992, Jordan helped the U.S. men's basketball team win the Olympic Games gold medal.

Write T in front of a true statement. Write N if it is not true.

_____ 1. A good title for this article would be, *All the Best Basketball Players.*

_____ 2. Michael played basketball in the city where he was born.

_____ 3. Michael's nickname was given to him because he jumps so high.

_____ 4. For several years, Michael played for the Chicago Bulls.

_____ 5. Jordan's middle name is Jonathan.

_____ 6. Michael played for the U.S. Olympic basketball team.

_____ 7. The article does not tell when he retired from playing basketball.

_____ 8. The article tells us that Jordan is famous for his long-range shots.

Name _____

Ball Parts

The word *basketball* is a compound word because it is made up of two smaller words, *basket* and *ball*. The game was first played by throwing a ball into a peach *basket*, rather than a hoop and a net, so that is how the game was named. Many other words you know are compound words. Draw a line between two words to make a compound word, and then draw a line to the picture it matches. Then color the pictures.

basket	fly
water	place
chalk	hopper
butter	board
news	ball
grass	corn
fire	melon
pop	walk
side	paper

Name _____

An Orange Basketball

Have you ever noticed that in many ways, a basketball is like an orange?
You probably know that the two are different in many ways, too.
When we think of how two things are alike, we *compare* them.
When we think of how two things are different, we *contrast* them.
Read each fact in the chart. Is it true of a basketball? An orange?
Both? Write an X in the column where it is true.

	Basketball	Orange
1. It is round.		
2. It can be orange in color.		
3. It bounces.		
4. It is good to eat.		
5. You can cut it in half and use only part of it at a time.		
6. You can use it over and over.		
7. It can come in many different colors.		
8. It rolls.		
9. It is made of rubber.		
10. Sometimes you have to put air in it.		

Name _____

Ordering numbers

Uniform Numbers

Did you know that in basketball, players never use a digit larger than 5?
That is because the referee has to identify each player by showing his number
with his fingers. If the referee is signaling a player wearing number 35,
for example, the referee holds up first 3 fingers and then 5 fingers.
This system would not work very well if the player's number was 76 would it?

Shown here are some numbers that belong to the players on the Tigers team.
First write them in order from lowest to highest.

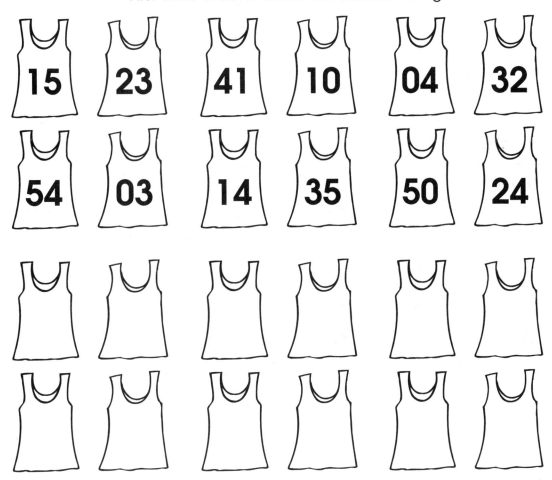

Now, think of some more numbers that the Tigers team could use on their uniforms:

Name _____

Score More

Here is a chart that shows how many points the players on the Tigers team scored in a game against the Lions. Read it carefully, and then answer the questions below.

Player's Name	Points Scored in the First Half	Points Scored in the Second Half
Sam Dunk	10	4
Ree Bound	6	12
Pete Jump	2	6
Ican Shoot	12	10
Kno Foul	7	11
Lee Ap	8	8

Write just the first names of the players in the blanks.

1. Who scored the most points in the first half? _____

2. Who scored the most points in the second half? _____

3. Who made the same amount of points in each half?

   _____

4. Who scored the most points altogether? _____

5. Who scored twice as many points in the second half as he or she did in the first

   half? _____

6. How many points did these six players score altogether in the first half of the

   game? _____

7. In the first half of the game, what two players together scored the same

   number of points as Lee? _____ and

   _____

Discovery of the South Pole

December 14 marks the anniversary of the discovery of the South Pole. That makes December a great time to teach your primary students about Antarctica, explorers, dogsleds and penguins.

Background Information

On December 14, 1911, Roald Amundsen of Norway became the first person to reach the mysterious spot that so many other explorers before him had tried to visit. With a team of four other men and 52 sled dogs, Amundsen successfully reached the Pole. All of the men and 12 of the dogs returned to their base camp safely.

The most famous explorer to Antarctica was probably Richard E. Byrd of the U.S. Navy's Operation High Jump. Thousands of men made surveys most of the way around the continent.

More recently, in 1990, a six-man international team led by American Will Steger finished a 221-day, 3700-mile trip across the continent using dogsleds. It was the longest dogsled trek, and the first "unmechanized passage" through the South Pole.

Amazingly, the only native land animals to Antarctica are arthropods (such as insects). Around the coasts, however, live seals, penguins and about 45 other species of birds. The penguins are great swimmers and catch their food (a shrimp-like animal called krill and fish) underwater.

Explore the activities on the pages that follow to lead your students through some number, reading and *thinking* fun. Also consider bundling up your students with their hats, coats, boots and mittens to explore winter *outside* your classroom.

Matching
Mitten Matchup

The air is very cold all the time at the South Pole, and explorers must dress in very warm clothes. Imagine that a group of explorers have thrown all of their mittens into one big pile. Find all the pairs by drawing a line between each matching set. You will have one odd mitten left over. Circle the extra mitten. Color all the rest.

Name _____

Dogsled Numbers

The person who first discovered the South Pole traveled by dogsled.
Look at this big dogsled. How many dogs are pulling it? Count by twos to find out.
Write the number under each pair.

Name _____

Teacher: Read this poem aloud with your students. Ask them to hold up the right number of fingers for each line. They may also want to add other appropriate actions.
Use the poem with the language activity on the next page.

Countdown action poem

Ten Little Penguins

Ten little penguins sitting in a line.
One swam away, and then there were nine.

Nine little penguins learning how to skate.
One fell down, and then there were eight.

Eight little penguins—one was named Devin.
He lost his mitten, and then there were seven.

Seven little penguins learning lots of tricks.
One bumped his head, and then there were six.

Six little penguins ready for a dive.
One took a dip, and then there were five.

Five little penguins resting on the shore.
One fell asleep, and then there were four.

Four little penguins waddling by the sea.
One slipped in, and then there were three.

Three little penguins wondering what to do.
One went home, and then there were two.

Two little penguins looking for some fun.
One went to lunch, and then there was one.

One little penguin standing all alone.
He jumped in the water, and now there are none!

Number words, rhyming words

Rhyme Time

Look at the "Ten Little Penguins" poem. Can you find each number word and the word that rhymes with it? For each word below, find a number word and another word that rhymes with it. Copy the words from the poem. An example is done for you.

	Number Word	**Other Word**
A. gate	eight	skate
B. Kevin		
C. mine		
D. run		
E. more		
F. mix		
G. me		
H. hive		
I. shoe		

Read the poem again. Underline all the number words.

Following directions

Treasure Hunt

Pretend you are in search of the South Pole. You know it is marked with an X, but which one? Follow the directions to find the correct X. Circle it with a red crayon. Good luck!

1. Start at the X in the top left corner.

2. Move down two lines.

3. Move over to the right three Xs.

4. Move up one X.

5. Move to the left 2 Xs.

6. Move down 4 rows.

7. Move to the right to the end of that row.

8. Move up 2 rows. Circle the X. You've just found the South Pole!

X X X X X X

X X X X X X

X X X X X X

X X X X X X

X X X X X X

X X X X X X

Name _____

Find It on the Map

Where is the South Pole? To find out, look at a globe. A globe is a model of the Earth.
It is the same shape as our planet. When you look at the front of the globe,
you can only see half of it. You must turn it to see the other half.
Here are maps that show two sides of a globe.

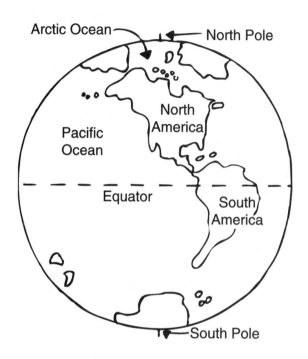
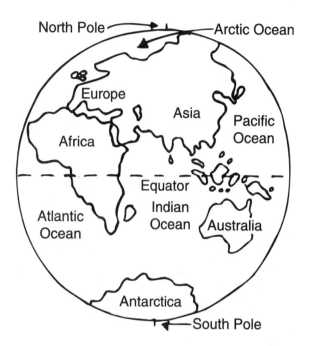

1. To find the South Pole, look for the large piece of land called *Antarctica*.
   Antarctica is one of the seven continents of the world. The South Pole is at the very
   bottom, in the center of the globe. Draw a red X on the South Pole on both maps.

2. Next look at the other continents. Follow these directions:
   ✎ The United States, Canada and Mexico are in North America. Draw a blue X on
   this continent.
   ✎ Brazil, Colombia and Chile are some of the countries in South America. Color
   this continent yellow.
   ✎ In Europe you can find England, Ireland, France and Italy. Draw a green X on
   Europe.
   ✎ In Asia you can find China and part of Russia. Draw an orange X on Asia.
   ✎ In Australia you can find koalas and kangaroos. Color Australia with your brown
   crayon.
   ✎ Some of the countries in Africa are Egypt, Libya and Somalia. Draw a yellow X
   on Africa.

3. Now find the North Pole. It is not on a continent. It is at the very top of the globe,
   exactly opposite from the South Pole. Find this spot on both maps. Draw a red N on
   the spot that marks the North Pole.

Resources

Antarctica by Helen Cowcher. Milit Publishing, Limited, 1997.

North Pole, South Pole by Jacques Duquennoy. Raincoast Book Distribution, 2001.

Penguins! by Gail Gibbons. Holiday House, Inc., 1998.

The Penguin, a Funny Bird by Beatrice Fontanel. Charlesbridge Publishing, Inc., 1992.

Penguin Pete by Marcus Pfister. North-South Books, 1993.

Plenty of Penguins (Hello Reader! Science Series) by Sonia W. Black. Scholastic, 2000.

Some Folks Think the South Pole's Hot: The Three Tenors Play the Antarctic by Elke Heidenreich, et al. David R. Godine, 2001.

Tacky the Penguin by Helen Lester. Houghton Mifflin Co., 1990.

A Wish for Wings That Work: An Opus Christmas Story by Berkeley Breathed. Little, Brown, & Co., 1995 (reissue).

Book and Cassette

Ice Continent: A Story of Antarctica by Louise A. Young. Soundprints, 1997.

Don't forget the classic, *Mr. Popper's Penguins,* by Richard and Florence Atwater, published by Little Brown & Company with various editions and copyright dates. It's also available on cassette. While the book is probably too difficult for your primary students to read on their own, you may wish to read portions of it to them.

Hanukkah

Hanukkah, often called the Festival of Lights, is a Jewish holiday. It is observed as a reminder of the miracle that happened long ago to celebrate the freeing of the Jewish temple from its defilement by the Greeks. Tradition says that when the small band of Jewish Maccabees won the battle against the Greeks and reclaimed their temple, they wanted to light a lamp there. There was only enough oil to burn a lamp for one night, but miraculously, the lamp remained lit for eight days. So Hanukkah has come to be an eight-day celebration of the miracle of the light as well as the victory of the Maccabees.

With that history in mind, consider celebrating this special season with your students with the skill reproducibles that follow. Also, try making some of these Jewish Hanukkah recipes with your students.

Potato Latkes

This traditional Hanukkah food is sure to be a hit with your students. Prepare the potatoes at home to save time in class. Be sure you have an extra adult on hand to operate the electric frying pan and to keep kids away from the hot oil!

5 or 6 medium potatoes, scrubbed, peeled and grated
1 medium onion, grated
2 eggs, beaten
1/2 tsp. pepper
1/2 tsp. salt
3 tablespoons bread crumbs or crushed crackers
1/4 cup oil for frying

Peel and grate the potatoes. If desired, you can do this at home the night before. Cover the grated potatoes with water and place in refrigerator over night. In the morning, put potatoes in a strainer to drain away as much liquid as possible. Place beaten eggs, seasonings and crumbs in a large bowl. Add onions and well-drained potatoes and mix well. Preheat electric frying pan to 350°F. Add oil. When the oil is hot, add one large tablespoon of batter for each pancake. Cook 4-5 minutes on one side. Flip, and cook another 4 minutes. Serve hot with a dish of cold applesauce.

Candle Cookie Cupcakes

With only three main ingredients, the measuring and mixing are a breeze. Make this recipe for Hanukkah, Christmas, birthdays or any other special celebration that features candles. This recipe makes about 24 cupcakes.

28 cream-filled chocolate sandwich cookies
6 tablespoons butter, unsalted if possible
1 quart ice cream or frozen yogurt, any flavor

Other materials and equipment: food processor, saucepan or small microwavable bowl, muffin/cupcake pans, large spoon, Hanukkah candles.

Teacher: To prepare ingredients for the crust, place 24 of the cookies in a food processor and grind until very fine. Melt the butter in a small saucepan or microwave and mix well with the cookies.

Students: Wash hands thoroughly. Put one paper cupcake liner in each muffin mold. Using fingers, press some of the cookie-butter mixture along the bottom and up the sides of each cupcake liner. Try to get the mixture pressed together as smoothly and evenly as possible. Take the ice cream or frozen yogurt from the freezer and let it soften for a few minutes. Then spoon it into the cupcake papers. Fill the papers and press down until ice cream or yogurt is smooth.

Place the filled cupcake pans in the freezer until the cupcakes hold together well, or about three hours.

Insert a Hanukkah candle into the center of each cupcake. Refreeze until treats are very solid, and wrap well. *(Note: All preparations up until this point may be done up to a week in advance.)*

Arrange the cupcakes as desired. If you choose to make a menorah, arrange eight of the cupcakes in one line. Put the ninth candle, the *shamash*, in the middle, but raise it higher than the others by placing it on top of the extra sandwich cookies. Light the candles immediately, but be sure to blow them out before the ice cream gets soft!

For other occasions, put the candles in a circle or star pattern, or simply arrange them on a serving tray.

Observing details
Michael's Candles

Michael is looking for his Hanukkah candles. Can you help him?
He needs to find 8 small candles and 1 large candle to place in his menorah.
Circle the candles that you find. Color the picture.

Name _____

Getting Ready for Hanukkah

Read these sentences about Hanukkah.
Write the word in the blank that has a long vowel sound.

1. Is that a _____ I see?

    cake   gift   net

2. Don't you _____ the holidays?

    miss   think   like

3. We _____ some gifts.

    took   gave   bought

4. It is really _____ to play with the dreidel!

    fun   neat   sad

5. When can we _____ the food?

    cook   eat   share

6. Let's _____ together.

    work   play   come

Name _____

Hanukkah Hunt

Hanukkah is a Jewish celebration that lasts for eight days. It reminds folks of the time when the ancient Maccabees fought for their survival (and their temple) and won. It reminds them of the time when there was only enough oil in their temple lamp for one day and it lasted for eight days. Today, Jewish people celebrate Hanukkah by lighting candles in the menorah, giving gifts, eating special foods, playing a game with a spinning dreidel and spending time with their families. You may see symbols, such as the Star of David, and other decorations in blue and white.

Find the Hanukkah words listed in the box in the puzzle below.
Words can go up and down, across or diagonally.

W	X	E	L	P	M	E	T
H	A	K	K	U	N	A	H
I	J	R	A	T	S	E	G
T	E	Q	H	L	U	I	I
E	W	G	I	L	F	X	L
Q	I	O	B	T	Q	A	V
E	S	Y	L	I	M	A	F
Z	H	V	Q	P	W	Q	O
C	A	N	D	L	E	S	O
X	L	E	D	I	E	R	D

blue
candles
dreidel
eight
family
food
gift
Hanukkah
Jewish
lamp
light
oil
star
temple
white

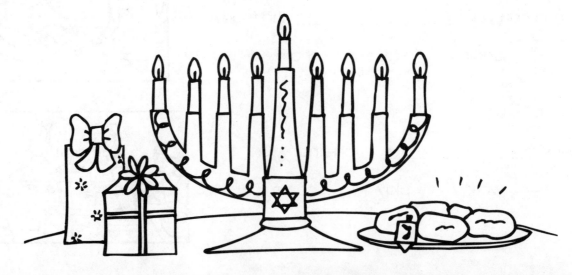

Name _____

The Main Idea

The main idea is what a story is about. The other sentences give details that tell more about the main idea. Read this story. Then circle the main idea. Underline the details. At the bottom of the page, draw a picture that matches the story.

A menorah is an important part of Hanukkah. It is a special candle holder. It has eight branches for the smaller candles and a ninth holder for the bigger candle. The big candle is called a shamash.

Every night during Hanukkah, the family gathers around the menorah. On the first night, the shamash is lit. Then it is used to light the first of the small candles. On the second night the shamash is used to light the first two candles, and on the third night, it is used to light three candles and so on. Two blessings are said each night; one is a blessing over the candles, and the other is in memory of the miracle of the temple oil.

The menorah is put in a window where everyone can see it. It is a special symbol for a special time.

Draw your picture here.

Cut and paste, finding sets of eight
Eight Days of Dominoes?

You may know that *eight* is an important number during December. The Jewish Hanukkah celebration lasts for eight days. Count all the dots on these dominoes. Cut out only the pieces that have exactly eight dots. Paste them on another piece of paper.

Number patterns

Spin, Dreidel, Spin!

A dreidel is a Jewish toy with four sides that is spun like a top in a game. Look where these dreidels have been spinning! Start at each toy and trace its path with your finger. Fill in the numbers that are missing in each pattern.

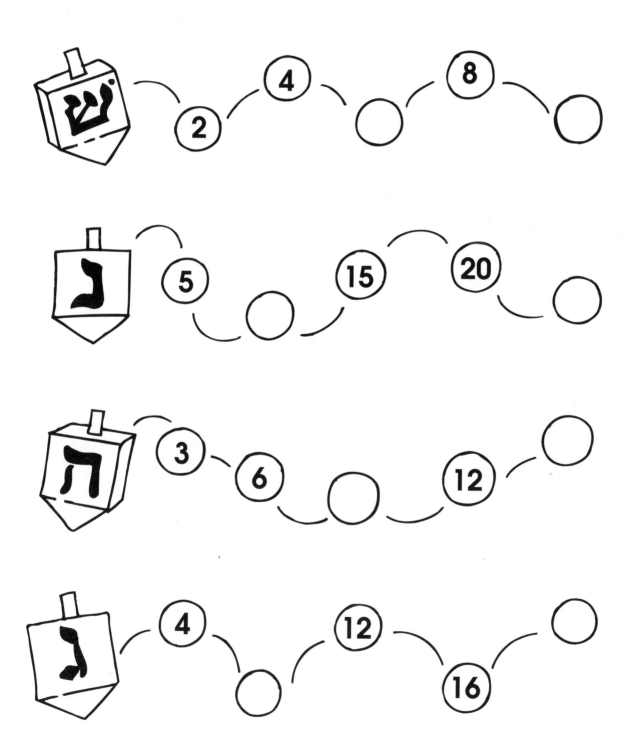

Name _____

Eights Are Great!

Hanukkah is a special eight-day celebration.
It's a great time to write math problems with the answer of 8.

Here is an addition problem where the answer is 8: $6 + 2 = 8$

Write five more addition problems that have 8 for an answer.

1. _____

2. _____

3. _____

4. _____

5. _____

Here is a subtraction problem where the answer is 8: $12 - 4 = 8$

Write five more subtraction problems that have 8 for an answer.

1. _____

2. _____

3. _____

4. _____

5. _____

Now find the answers to these problems with the number 8.

A. $88 - 8 =$ _____

B. $888 - 8 =$ _____

C. $88 + 8 =$ _____

D. $888 + 8 =$ _____

284

Christmas

Make the most of the joy of Christmas by introducing your students to the festive reproducibles in this section. They can enjoy this favorite holiday while they practice their observation, language and math skills. You'll also find a bulletin board, gift tags and a shape book on the pages that follow.

Santa Claus, wish lists and Christmas shopping are key elements of the season. Try your hand at shifting students' attention from receiving gifts to giving gifts with these simple make-at-school gift ideas:

- Cookies in a Jar (page 288)

- Christmas Gift Coupons (page 289)

- Handmade Greeting Cards and Bookmarks: Let students draw their own designs or use holiday clip art to create customized cards and bookmarks for their family members. Be sure to have plenty of colored paper, markers, glitter, glue and sequins on hand.

- Puzzle Piece Photo Frames: Cut out the back of the frame from a cereal box. On the plain side of the piece, center and glue a picture of the student. Paint some pieces from an old jigsaw puzzle in red tempera paint; paint other pieces in green. Let them dry. Then glue the red and green pieces around the photo as a decorative Christmas frame. Cover the back of the frame with gift wrap.

- Handprint Place Mats: Start with green poster board, cut to the size of an ordinary place mat, about 12" x 15". Paint students' hands with red tempera paint. Have them press hands firmly in the middle of the mat. Let handprints dry. Cover place mat with clear, self-adhesive paper. If you like, have each student make a second mat in reverse colors (green handprints on red poster board) so that he can take home a pair of place mats.

What holiday season could be complete without a classroom party? Simple snack ideas include:

- Red and green finger gelatin cut-outs: For each color of gelatin treats desired, mix $2^1/2$ cups boiling water with 4 small packages of gelatin (regular or sugar free). Pour into a 9" x 13" pan. Chill until firm. Cut out with Christmas cookie cutters.

- Vegetable Kabobs: Use toothpicks as skewers. Layer cherry tomatoes with chunks of celery and green peppers for a healthy red and green treat.

- Jelly Sandwiches: Use cookie cutters to cut any type of sliced bread into Christmas shapes. Spread with red raspberry, cherry or strawberry jam for red open-faced sandwiches. Or spread with mint apple jelly for green ones.

- Holly Green Punch: Combine 2 packages of lime-flavored drink, 2 cups sugar, 2 quarts of cold water, 1 46-oz. can of chilled pineapple juice and 2 liters of chilled ginger ale. (For Jolly Red Punch, substitute cherry or strawberry-flavored drink in place of the lime.)

- Build festive, edible scenes with fruit-flavored gumdrops, raisins, chocolate and butterscotch chips and marshmallows. Challenge students to build a Christmas tree, a sleigh, a snowman or a reindeer with these and similar ingredients. After displaying original designs, instruct the creators to indulge!

Here is a very simple, yet colorful bulletin board idea for your holiday classroom.

Cut letters for *Merry Christmas from . . .* the fronts of old Christmas cards. Use more card fronts to form a border for this colorful bulletin board.

Ask each student to cut out a gift tag (page 287). He should write his name on it and color it. Use inexpensive stick-on bows to form the Christmas tree. Let each student select a bow, and then attach his homemade gift tag to it with thread.

Note: For extra durability, carefully staple each bow to the bulletin board. Allow students to add construction paper "gifts" under the tree and additional decorations as they choose.

Gift Tags

Use these gift tags for the bulletin board on page 286 and for gifts
students may want to give to each other or to their family members.

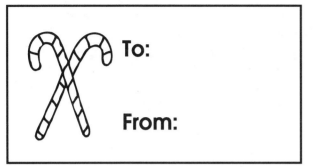
To:

From:

To:

From:

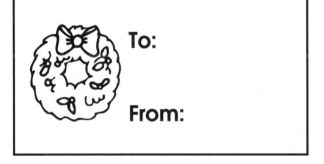
To:

From:

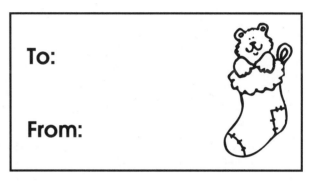
To:

From:

To:

From:

To:

From:

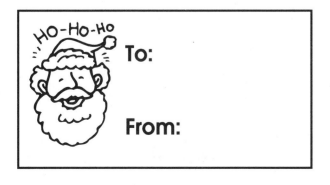
To:

From:

To:

From:

Cookies in a Jar

Preparations

For this gift, each child will need a clean one-quart jar and lid. You and/or volunteers will need to supply sugar, brown sugar, flaked coconut, chopped pecans, walnuts or macadamia nuts, chopped dates or raisins, flour, baking soda and baking powder. Before students begin to assemble the contents of their jars, make a batch of this mixture for each student:

 2 cups flour
 1 teaspoon baking soda
 1 teaspoon baking powder

Assembly

Instruct students to assemble these layers in the order given. They should press each layer firmly in place before adding the next ingredient.

 $1/3$ cup sugar
 $1/2$ cup packed brown sugar
 $1/3$ cup packed flaked coconut
 $2/3$ cup chopped nuts (pecans, walnuts or macadamia nuts)
 $2/3$ cup chopped dates or raisins
 2 cups flour mixed with 1 tsp. baking soda and 1 tsp. baking powder

Put lid tightly on jar. Place a piece of Christmas fabric or tissue paper on the lid and tie it in place with yarn or raffia.

Print these directions and tie to the jar or glue to the front.

Cookies in a Jar

Empty cookie mix into large mixing bowl. Stir to combine ingredients. Add $1/2$ cup softened butter or margarine, 1 egg (slighly beaten) and 1 teaspoon vanilla. Mix until completely blended. Roll dough into walnut-sized balls. Place 2" apart on a lightly greased cookie sheet. Press cookie down slightly with the heel of your hand. Bake at 350°F for 11-13 minutes or until edges are lightly browned. Cool 5 minutes on the baking sheet. Move to wire racks to cool completely. Makes about $2 1/2$ dozen.

Christmas Gift Coupons

This coupon is good for
10 hugs

To: _____

From: _____

Offer good on any day.

This coupon is good for
5 kisses

To: _____

From: _____

Offer good on any day.

Present this coupon, and I will
set the table

To: _____

From: _____

Offer good on any day.

Present this coupon, and I will
set the table

To: _____

From: _____

Offer good on any day.

This coupon is good for
breakfast in bed

To: _____

From: _____

Offer good on any day.

Present this coupon, and I will
clean my room

To: _____

From: _____

Offer good on any day.

This coupon is good for
_____

To: _____

From: _____

Offer good on any day.

Present this coupon, and I will
_____

To: _____

From: _____

Offer good on any day.

Shape Book Pattern

The alphabet

Christmas Stockings

Each stocking is missing one letter of the alphabet. Can you find out what it is? Write the missing letter under each stocking. The letters will spell the name of a Christmas shape.

Answer: ____ ____ ____ ____

_____

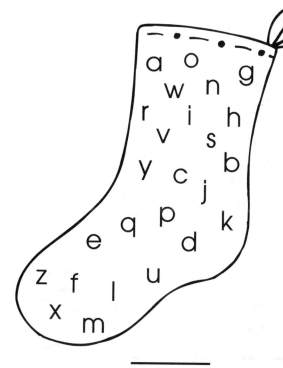

_____

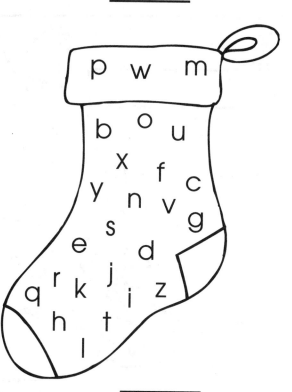

_____

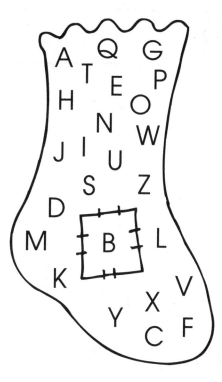

_____

Noting and reproducing visual details

Keeping Watch

It's Christmas Eve, and these three children are keeping watch for Santa Claus.
Do you think they will see him? Write your name on the fireplace.
Then find the 10 missing things in the bottom picture and draw them in.

Name _____

Three in a Row

Look at these tic-tac-toe boards that show Christmas items. On each one,
find the three that are exactly the same. Draw a line to show the three in a row.
The row can go up, down, across or diagonally.

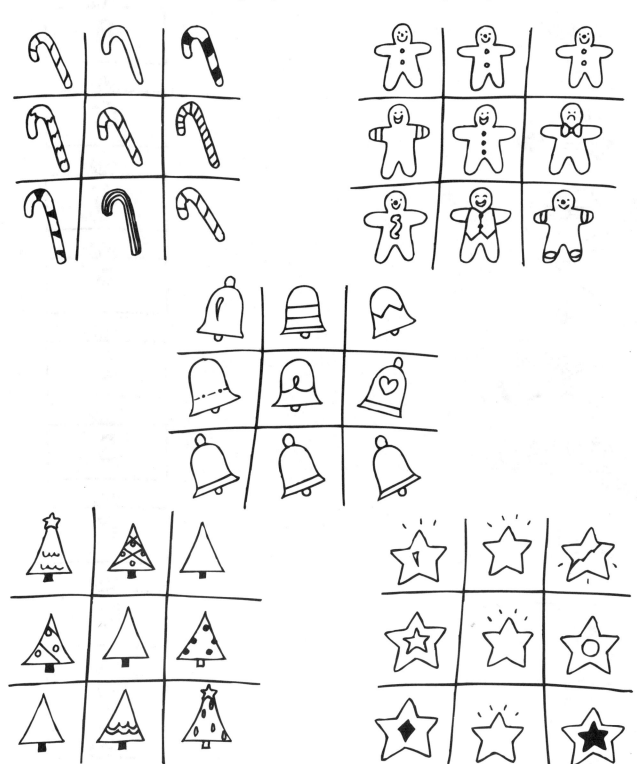

Beginning consonants
Letter Gifts

Match each gift to the correct box. Draw a line from the
gift to the box that shows the first letter in the name of the gift.

B

C

W

P

L

S

K

M

D

G

Name _____

ABC order

Wanda's Wish List

Wanda has a very long wish list! She knows, of course, that she won't receive everything on her list, but she likes to give Santa lots of ideas. Wanda thinks she should write all of her ideas in ABC order before she sends her list to Santa. Number the words from 1 to 15 to show how they should be in ABC order. Then write the list again in order.

_____ wallet

_____ horse

_____ sweater

_____ candle

_____ train

_____ football

_____ knitting needles

_____ yarn

_____ birdhouse

_____ robe

_____ puppy

_____ goldfish

_____ quilt

_____ jeans

_____ dictionary

1. _____

2. _____

3. _____

4. _____

5. _____

6. _____

7. _____

8. _____

9. _____

10. _____

11. _____

12. _____

13. _____

14. _____

15. _____

Identifying sentence parts

Christmas Parts

Remember that every sentence has two parts.
The *subject* is the naming part. It tells who or what the sentence is about.
The *predicate* is the telling part. It tells what the subject does or did.
Read these sentences about a Christmas play. Follow the directions.

A. Write the subject on the line.

1. Mary has the part of the angel. _____

2. Mrs. Smith decided who would act out each part. _____

3. The whole school wants to see our play. _____

4. We are practicing every day. _____

B. Write the predicate on the line.

5. Jody and Randy are shepherds. _____

6. They make funny sheep sounds! _____

7. The principal will come to see our play. _____

8. Mike's mom made our costumes. _____

C. Draw lines to match the sentence parts.

Subjects	**Predicates**
9. The room where we will have the play	fits just right.
10. All the students	will play her flute.
11. My costume	have invited their parents.
12. Sarah	has lots of seats.

Writing compound sentences
Giving Gifts

You can join two sentences that tell about related ideas.

* Use *and* to join sentences with similar ideas.
  John likes to read. Jane likes to write.
  John likes to read, and Jane likes to write.

* Use *but* to join sentences with different ideas.
  Mom likes coconut. Dad doesn't.
  Mom likes coconut but Dad doesn't.

Read these sentences about Christmas. Join them using *and* or *but*.

1. Sis likes gingerbread cookies. Sam likes butter cookies better.

_____

_____

2. Ann's stocking is green. Amy's stocking is red.

_____

_____

3. My favorite part of Christmas is giving gifts. Dad's favorite part is opening them!

_____

_____

4. Reindeer have antlers. Horses do not.

_____

_____

5. I can't sleep on Christmas Eve. Neither can my brother.

_____

_____

Classification
Sort It Out

Read the headings of the three groups below. Write each word from the word box under the correct heading. One has been done for you.

~~gingerbread~~	bicycle	lights	star
wreath	oranges	teddy bear	board game
cookies	ham	grapes	ribbon
bells	doctor's kit	holly	
doll	turkey	dump truck	

Food	Christmas Decorations	Toys
gingerbread	_____	_____
_____	_____	_____
_____	_____	_____
_____	_____	_____
_____	_____	_____

Name _____

Counting, solving word problems
O Christmas Tree!

Read each question. Look at the picture. Write your answers in the blanks.

1. How many bells are on the tree? _____
   Draw 2 more bells. Now how many are there? _____

2. How many gifts are under the tree? _____
   Cross out 3 gifts. Now how many are there? _____

3. How many stockings do you see? _____
   Draw 4 more stockings. Now how many are there? _____

4. How many bows do you see on the floor? _____
   Cross out 5 bows. Now how many bows are there? _____

5. How many candy canes are on the tree? _____
   Draw 4 more candy canes. Now how many are there? _____

Using coordinates

Boxing Match

Which box contains each Christmas ornament? Write the coordinates of each shape.
The first one is done for you.

	1	**2**	**3**	**4**
A				
B				
C				
D				

 1. __3B__

 2. _____

 3. _____

 4. _____

 5. _____

 6. _____

 7. _____

 8. _____

 9. _____

Name _____

Charity Gifts

Jill's class collected money for the needy at Christmastime. The boxes show the coins that were collected each day. How many cents are in each box?

Remember: A nickel = five cents (5¢)

 A dime = ten cents (10¢)

Monday

_____ ¢

Tuesday

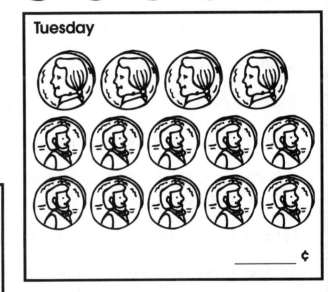

_____ ¢

Wednesday

_____ ¢

Friday

_____ ¢

Thursday

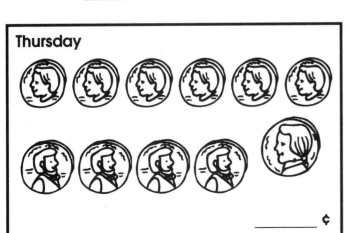

_____ ¢

Kwanzaa

Kwanzaa was created in 1966 by Dr. Maulana Karenga. He wanted African Americans to have a holiday that made them feel proud of their heritage and their community.

Kwanzaa is a week-long celebration. Each night features a different theme. These are:

    December 26—Unity
    December 27—Self-determination
    December 28—Collective work and responsibility
    December 29—Cooperative economics
    December 30—Purpose
    December 31—Creativity
    January 1—Faith

To learn more about this holiday, check out some of these resources:

Crafts for Kwanzaa by Kathy Ross, et al. Millbrook Press, 1994.

The Gifts of Kwanzaa by Synthia Saint James. Albert Whitman, 1997.

Imani's Gift at Kwanzaa by Denise Burden-Patmon. Aladdin Paperbacks, 1992.

A Kwanzaa Celebration Pop-Up Book by Nancy Williams. Simon & Schuster Children's, 1995.

Let's Get Ready for Kwanzaa by Joanne Winne. Children's Press, 2001.

My First Kwanzaa Book by Deborah M. Newton Chocolate. Scholastic, 1999.

The Seven Days of Kwanzaa: How to Celebrate Them by Angela Shelf Medearis. Scholastic, 1994.

The Story of Kwanzaa by Donna L. Washington. HarperCollins Children's Books, 1997.

Together for Kwanzaa by Juwanda G. Ford, et al. Random House Books for Young Readers, 2000.

Spelling
String the Beads

Use a different color crayon to color the letters for each Kwanzaa word.
Use a black crayon to "string" each word together.

people	harvest	seven
candle	unity	faith

f

p

y

c

e

s

v

l

e

t

e

a

e

i

r

n

t

i

p

o

n

a

s

n

v

u

t

h

a

l

h

e

d

e

Recognizing and repoducing shapes

Kwanzaa Mat

The Kwanzaa symbols, such as corn, candles and fruit are placed on a mat.
Pretend this is a Kwanzaa mat. Look at the pieces in the mat. How many sides
does each piece have? Count them and write the number in the chart.
Then draw each piece three times. Try to make your drawing better each time.

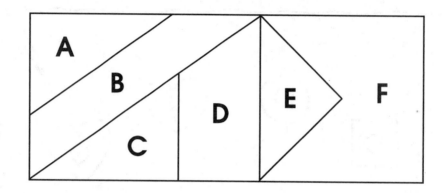

Shape	How many sides?	Draw each shape three times.
A		
B		
C		
D		
E		
F		

Bookmarks & Awards

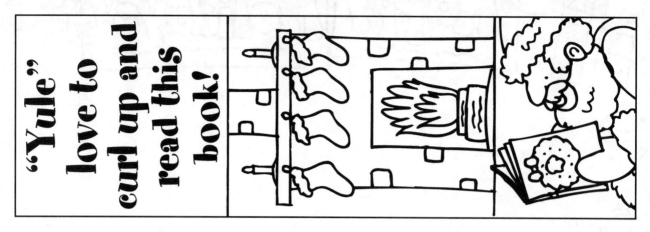

"Yule" love to curl up and read this book!

Hoop Hoop Hooray for Books!

This award goes to

_____

for

_____

You're "Tree"mendous!

Signed _____

Thanks,

_____,

for making my day so

SWEET!

Signed

_____

Answer Key

August

Race Pace, page 17

93, 100, 90, 92. Number 2 is the winner.

Shipshape, page 18

1. 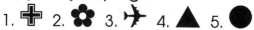 2. ✿ 3. ✈ 4. ▲ 5. ●

6. ▮ 7. ➡

Ferris Wheel Words, page 32

Long vowel words: beans, sheep, cake,
 tape, peach, goat, pie
Short vowel words: pet, pat, cap

What's the Next Word? page 41

1. pot
2. dog
3. party
4. tube
5. giving
6. mile
7. fair
8. leg
9. in
10. none

Can We Have a Title? page 54

1.c., 2. N, 3. T, 4. T, 5. N, 6. N, 7. T, 8. T

Capital Countries, page 56

1. Brazil
2. Cuba
3. Denmark
4. Egypt
5. France
6. Iran
7. Libya
8. Nigeria
9. Peru
10. Spain
11. Turkey
12. Yemen

Flag Tags, page 57

1. $60, 2. $37, 3. $35, 4. $45, 5. $24, 6.$48
7.$46, 8. $34

Skywriting, page 60

Y and Z

Airplane Graph, page 64

1. 6, 2. 5, 3. Jaun, 4. Sam, 5. yes, 6. yes,
7. Nikki, 8. 7

September

Hive Homes, page 71

Benji—3, Bailey—2, Bobby—4, Boris—1

Worker Bees, page 73

1. b.
2. 1
3. hive
4. by fanning their wings
5. c.
6. a.

Busy Bees! page 74

1. Worker bees begin to build . . .
2. The hive becomes larger . . .
3. The queen bee . . .
4. The eggs hatch . . .
5. The worker bees gather . . .
6. The workers bring . . .

Waiter, Waiter! page 85

1. customer, chair
2. customers, coats
3. person, menu
4. parents, highchair, page, crayons,
 children
5. drink, guest
6. coffee, tea, soda, water
7. milk, meal
8. cream, sugar, people, coffee, tea
9. person
10. meals, order, cook
11. guests, table

Answer Key

Order, Please! page 86

1. 11 eggs
2. 9 eggs
3. 20 eggs
4. 7 bowls of oatmeal
5. 12 sausages
6. 9 glasses orange juice
7. 9 glasses orange juice
8. 0 doughnuts

The Lunch Bunch, page 88

1. Maria
2. Tim
3. Dan
4. Rosa

Time for Change, page 98

Nick–10¢ 10¢ 10¢ 1¢ 1¢ = 32¢
Julia–25¢ 5¢ 5¢ 5¢ = 40¢
Josh–25¢ 25¢ 10¢ 5¢ = 65¢
Christie–10¢ 10¢ 5¢ 5¢ 1¢ = 31¢
Luke–25¢ 10¢ 5¢ 1¢ 1¢ = 42¢
Jacinda–5¢ 5¢ 5¢ 5¢ 1¢ = 21¢
Lisa–25¢ 25¢ 25¢ 1¢ = 76¢
Jacinda made the least.
Lisa made the most.

Grandma's House, page 106

17 circles
3 squares–4 if you count the frame of the picture
5 rectangles
13 triangles

Elephant Info, page 115

1. c.
2. a., c., d., e.
3. It has two nostrils on the end.
4. It sucks up water in its trunk; it squirts the water into its mouth.
5. fruit, shoots and leaves

October

Cookie, Please! page 131

ACROSS
2. green
3. speak
6. team
9. peep
10. flee
11. yield

DOWN
1. feet
2. geese
4. people
5. keep
7. eagle
8. money

Cookie Trail, page 135

Final answer: 2

A Stamp Story, page 141

1. c.
2. 8
3. Yes, she works on her collection every week.
4. her brother
5. saves stamps that come in the mail
6. cats and dogs
7. stamps about flags

Stamp Rhymes, page 142

1. damp
2. clamp
3. camp
4. lamp
5. ramp

Stuck on Stamps, page 145

1. 10¢, 2. 6¢, 3. 9¢, 4. 25¢, 5. 14¢,
6. 5¢, 7. 4¢

Stampwork, page 146

22 + 10
22 + 3
34 + 22
34 + 3
10 + 3
57 + 22
57 + 10
22 + 10 + 3
34 + 22 + 10

Answer Key

Go with the Flow, page 147

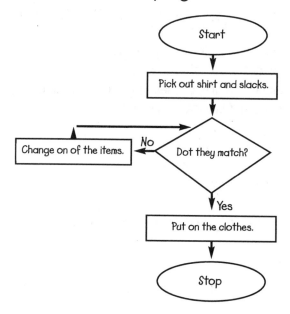

Fire Fighters, page 158
1. 24
2. 5
3. 3
4. 8
5. 14
6. 10
7. 20
8. 8
9. 190 feet
10. 9

Capital Idea! page 162
1. Christopher, Columbus, Genoa, Italy
2. Genoa, Europe
3. Genoa, India, China
4. Mediterranean, Sea
5. Europe, India
6. Christopher, Columbus, Portugal
7. Portugal, Columbus, Spain
8. King, Ferdinand, Queen Isabella, Spain, Columbus
9. Columbus, August, *Niña, Pinta, Santa Maria*
10. October, Columbus, San Salvador, North America

Sailing Search, page 163

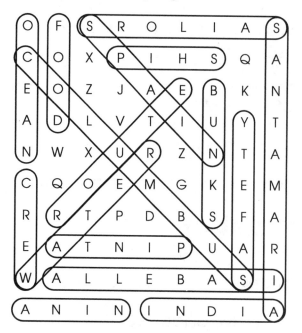

Race Pace, page 166
Santa Maria—14
Niña—10
Pinta—15
The *Niña* wins the race.

Dictionary Duty, page 171
A. 5, 3, 2, 4, 1
B. 4, 1, 3, 2, 5
C. 5, 2, 3, 4, 1
D. 4, 2, 1, 5, 3
E. 4, 3, 1, 2, 5
F. 4, 5, 3, 1, 2
G. 4, 5, 1, 2, 3
H. 4, 1, 5, 3, 2
I. 1, 2, 4, 5, 3

123, ABC, page 172
A. bake, best, bread
B. fine, freeze, fudge
C. hand, help, hip
D. jam, jelly, judge
E. zap, zip, zone
F. pest, prize, pump
G. gas, grease, guess
H. tack, toy, trick

Answer Key

Halloween Surprise, page 180

1. an orange kitten
2. in a box, with paper and ribbon
3. hot cereal
4. October
5. Mom
6. after school
7. she cooked his breakfast
   she gave him a gift
8. he thanked his mom for the gift
   he shared his candy with his mom

November

Tepees, page 192

35 triangles

Tepee Terms, page 195

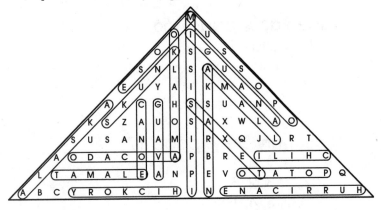

1. iguana, llama, moose, opossum, skunk
2. avocado, chili, guava, potato, tamale
3. Mississippi
4. Alaska, Mississippi, Nebraska, Oklahoma, Texas

A Look at the White House, page 202

(Answers may change depending on art.)

1. extra doorknob
2. extra window above door
3. one more bird on right
4. no curtains on left bottom window
5. missing window on right
6. zigzag trim on roof
7. extra flowers
8. extra bush on left
9. missing sidewalk

Read All About It! page 203

1. a.
2. b.
3. b.
4. c.
5. b.
6. b.

Count the Rooms, page 207

132

White House History, page 208

2, 12, 4, 6, 1, 8, 9, 5, 10, 3, 11, 7

ABC Ingredients, page 215

Rhymes: ham, jam

1. beef
2. cheese
3. eggs
4. fish
5. ham
6. jam
7. lettuce
8. mustard
9. nuts
10. onion
11. pickles
12. tomato

Plate Match, page 216

1. Kyle
2. Pete
3. Kelsie
4. Tasha

Answer Key

Sandwich Riddle, page 217
A submarine sandwich

Mayo's Monsters, page 218
1. squash and pickles
2. chili and cheese
3. chicken and rice
4. 3   (6 – 3)
5. ham and potato, onion and butter
6. 22 (6 + 10 + 6)
7. 29 (6 + 4 + 10 + 3 + 6)

Cover Story, page 230
1. A.
2. C.
3. B.
4. B.
5. A.

Overdue, page 234
1. 6¢
2. 10¢
3. 16¢
4. 18¢
5. 24¢
6. 12¢
7. 20¢
8. 40¢

Gobble, Gobble! page 239
B and D are the same.

Holiday Numbers, page 244
1. 7 pies
2. 30 oz.
3. 24 slices
4. 10 minutes
5. 5 pies
6. 24 pieces
7. 13 lbs.
8. 72 pieces

December

Basketball Barb, page 260
14 basketballs

Basketball Scramble, page 261
(Variations are also possible.)
1. The basketball net hangs from a rim.
2. A field goal is worth two points.
3. A free throw is worth one point.
4. The basketball court is a rectangle.
5. The ball is filled with air.
6. There are five players on a team.
7. Michael Jordan is a famous basketball player.

Read-Aloud Article, page 262
1. N, 2. N, 3. T, 4. T, 5. N, 6. T, 7. T, 8. N

Uniform Numbers, page 265
| 03 | 04 | 10 | 14 | 15 | 23 |
| 24 | 32 | 35 | 41 | 50 | 54 |

Many more numbers could be used such as 05, 11, 12, 13, 20, 21, 22, etc.

Score More, page 266
1. Ican
2. Ree
3. Lee
4. Ican
5. Ree
6. 45
7. Ree and Pete

Mitten Matchup, page 268

Treasure Hunt, page 272
The X to be circled is the last one to the right in the fourth row down from the top.

Answer Key

Hanukkah Hunt, page 280

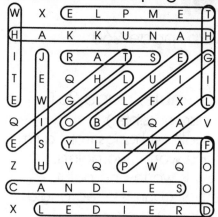

W	X	E	L	P	M	E	T
H	A	K	K	U	N	A	H
I	J	R	A	T	S	E	G
T	E	Q	H	L	U	I	I
E	W	G	I	L	F	X	L
Q	I	O	B	T	Q	A	V
E	S	Y	L	I	M	A	F
Z	H	V	Q	P	W	Q	O
C	A	N	D	L	E	S	O
X	L	E	D	I	E	R	D

Eights Are Great! page 284
A. 80, B. 880, C. 96, D. 896

Christmas Stockings, page 291
STAR

Keeping Watch, page 292
moon
face of clock
one stocking
star on tree
cat
one log from fireplace
mug
present
candle
girls ponytail

Wanda's Wish List, page 295
1. birdhouse
2. candle
3. dictionary
4. football
5. goldfish
6. horse
7. jeans
8. knitting needles
9. puppy
10. quilt
11. robe
12. sweater
13. train
14. wallet
15. yarn

Christmas Parts, page 296
1. Mary
2. Mrs. Smith
3. The whole school
4. We
5. are shepherds
6. make funny sheep sounds
7. will come to see our play
8. made our costumes
9. The room where we will have the play has lots of seats.
10. All the students have invited their parents.
11. My costume fits just right.
12. Sarah will play her flute.

Giving Gifts, page 297
(Variations are possible.)
1. Sis likes gingerbread cookies, but Sam likes butter cookies better.
2. Ann's stocking is green, and Amy's stocking is red.
3. My favorite part of Christmas is giving gifts, but Dad's favorite part is opening them!
4. Reindeer have antlers, but horses do not.
5. I can't sleep on Christmas Eve, and neither can my brother.

O Christmas Tree! page 299
1. 4, 6
2. 7, 4
3. 2, 6
4. 9, 4
5. 3, 7

Boxing Match, page 300
2. 2A
3. 1C
4. 2D
5. 4A
6. 1A
7. 3A
8. 2B
9. 3D

Charity Gifts, page 301
Monday: 53¢, Tuesday: 30¢, Wednesday: 52¢, Thursday: 69¢, Friday: 67¢

312

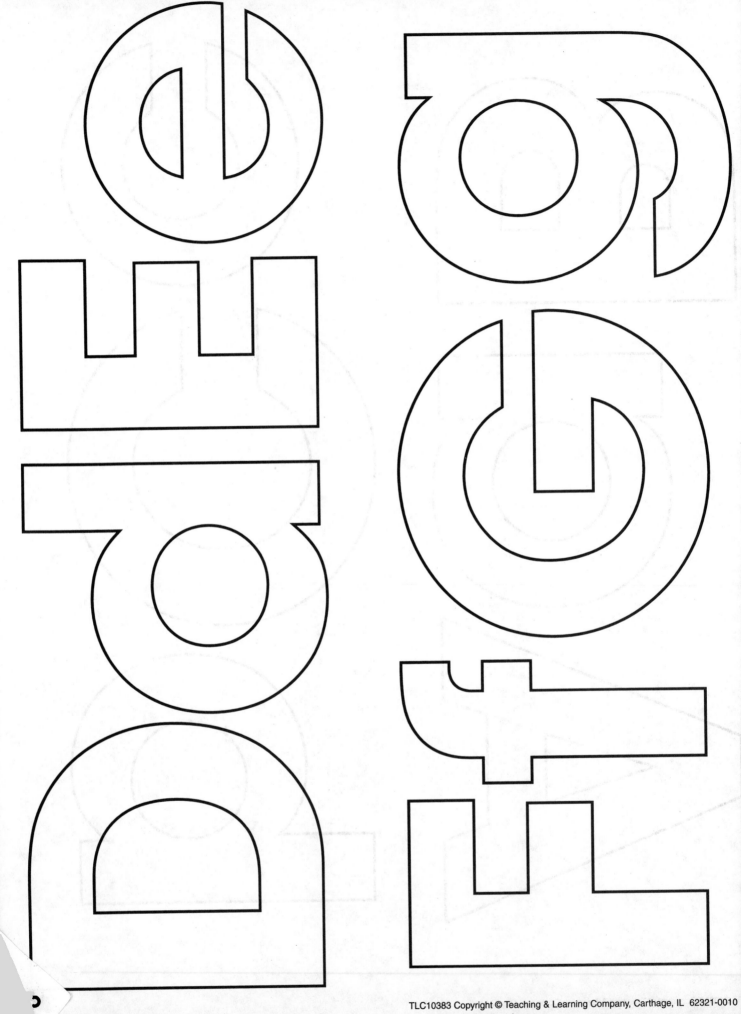

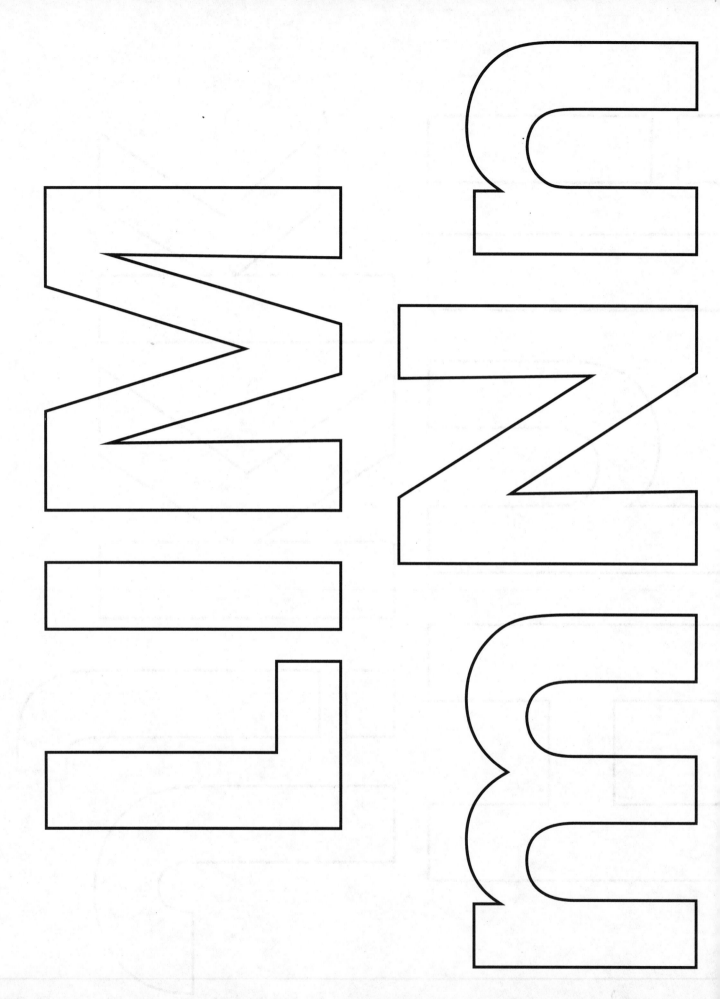

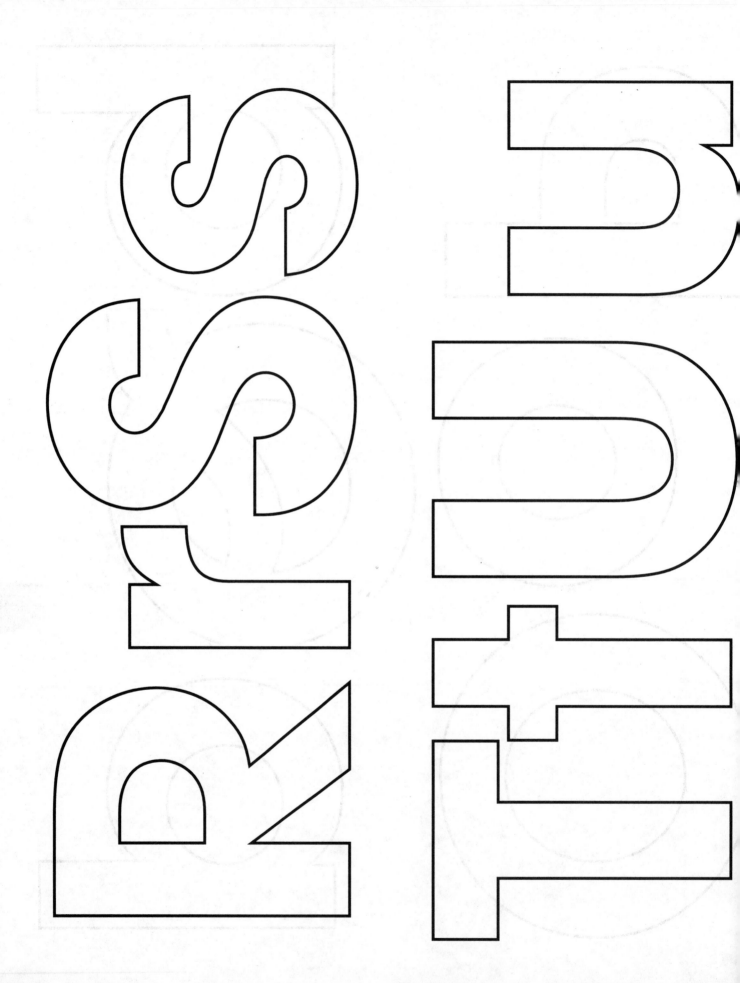

320